I0748510

DRAMATIC SCENES.

WITH OTHER POEMS,

NOW FIRST PRINTED.

BY

BARRY CORNWALL,

AUTHOR OF "ENGLISH SONGS," ETC.

BOSTON:
TICKNOR AND FIELDS.
M DCCC LVII.

CAMBRIDGE:

THURSTON AND TORRY, PRINTERS.

PREFACE.

Of the following "Dramatic Scenes," some were written thirty, and the others forty years ago: the first six scenes (published in 1819 and 1820) being now materially condensed and altered.

The Miscellaneous Poems, constituting "Part the Third" in the present volume, have never been before printed. With the exception of three small pieces of verse, they bear date many years back. They have, however, been corrected, in some instances completed, more recently.

In all probability, this book is the last with which I shall try the patience of the Public.

At one time, I — in common with other lovers of the charming Art of Poesy — prepared myself to enter those lists, where the Muses are said to award a wreath to each of the bolder combatants; but a long life of labor (my destiny) ensued, presenting few intervals of leisure, and forcing my thoughts into another course.

If years have not "brought the philosophic mind," they have at least quelled those aspirations which are troublesome only to the young; and I now feel that I ought to disburthen myself from my armor, and leave to more active and heroic spirits, the glory of the struggle, and the crown that awaits success.

B. W. PROCTER.

CONTENTS.

PART THE FIRST.

DRAMATIC SCENES.

PART THE SECOND.

DRAMATIC SCENES.

PART THE THIRD.

MISCELLANEOUS POEMS.

MISCELLANEOUS POEMS—*continued.*

MISCELLANEOUS POEMS — *continued.*

Part the First.

LUDOVICO SFORZA.

I'll close mine eyes,
And in a melancholy thought I'll frame
Her figure 'fore me. Now I have it — how strong
Imagination works! how she can frame
Things which are not! methinks she stands afore me.

WEBSTER — *The White Devil, Act III.*

Evad. Stay, sir, stay:
You are too hot, and I have brought you physic
To temper your high veins.
King. Thou dost not mean this; 'tis impossible:
Thou art too sweet and gentle.
Evad. No, I am not.

BEAUMONT AND FLETCHER — *The Maid's*
[*Tragedy, Act V.*

LUDOVICO SFORZA.

[This scene is founded partly on a fact in Italian history. Ludovico Sforza, uncle of the young Duke of Milan, was present at his marriage with Isabella, grand-daughter of the King of Naples. Sforza was much struck with the beauty of Isabella; and it was supposed that he caused his nephew, Galeazzo, to be poisoned. The last scene, which occurs after the lapse of a year, is imaginary.]

SCENE I.—*A Street.*

DUKE OF MILAN. LUDOVICO SFORZA.

DUKE.

And this proud lady, was she chaste as fair?

SFORZA.

Pure as the flame that burnt on Dian's altar,
And lovely as the morning. Oh! she shone
Like one of those bright shapes of fabling Greece,
(Born of the elements,) which, as men tell,
Wooed mortals to their arms. A form more beautiful,

Houri or child o' the air, ne'er glanced upon
A poet's dream, nor in Arabian story
Gave promise of their vaunted paradise.
Then, her voice was sweet
And tuned to music, bearing with it a charm,
Like numbers floating from the breathed flute,
Caught afar off, — and which the idle winds
Of June, through wantonness at evening, fling
O'er banks and beds of flowers.

DUKE.

And she is dead?

[ISABELLA *appears at a window.*

SFORZA.

Dead, dead! No; what is this? quick, tell me, sir.
Yon vision?

DUKE.

Uncle, look upon her, — there.

SFORZA.

I see: the grave gives up its habitant.
It is herself, — her shadow. Can the eye
Resume its lustre, after death has drawn
His filmy veil around it? Look!

DUKE.

My lord?

SFORZA.

She's vanished.

[ISABELLA *leaves the window.*

DUKE.

'Tis Isabella, sir ; my bride.

SFORZA.

Your bride ?
She's very fair. I've seen the face before ;
Dreamed of it — somewhere : where ? I know not where.
I'll dream no more, but think ; and act, — perhaps.

Enter ISABELLA *attended;* PIERO DE MEDICI, *and others.*

DUKE.

My Isabella ! you have rested well,
After your journey ? well ? Fatigue seems loth
To harm you ; and your eyes are spared, I see,
For many a Milan conquest.

ISABELLA.

There's but one
My duty bids me look to.

DUKE.

And your heart ?

ISABELLA.

And — and my heart.

DUKE.

Come hither! a few words ——

[*They talk aside.*

DE MEDICI.

My lord, my lord!

SFORZA.

Ha! my De Medici! welcome.

DE MEDICI.

Thanks, dear Sforza;
Are you so wrapped in dreams you miss your friends?

SFORZA.

No; 'tis my nephew, in a fairy dream,
Forgets me.

DUKE.

My dear uncle, pardon, pardon.
This is my guardian, dearest Isabel:
My father, I should say: I pray you love him.

SFORZA.

Ludovico Sforza, lady, and your knight;
If you will own so poor a one.

ISABELLA.

Thanks, sir.

DUKE.

Look! Those are the Alps, my love.

SFORZA.

Ay; turn your eyes
Here, madam. Look! methinks their snowy crowns
Shine radiantly as they had seen the sun.

DUKE.

The very hills give welcome to my love;
And every thing seems happy now, but most
The heart of Milan.

ISABELLA.

You will spoil me, sir.

SFORZA.

This day looks like
The holiday of Nature, madam, and you
The queen of 't.

ISABELLA.

Pray, no more.

DUKE.

No more then. Come!
The heat will mar you: let us seek the shade.

SFORZA.

I'll follow. [*Exeunt.*
She's gone — and it is night. What! shall I in age
Sink into folly? and this puny boy
To cheat his tutor! It may please him now
To *reign* in Milan: no, no, that's my care.
Oh! what an eye she has. It is not likely
She will live quiet here: her look forbids it.
She will be Duke: and I —— Now had I been
The same Ludovico Sforza who did win,
Some twenty years ago, the prize at Florence,
Perhaps she might have loved me. Love? — that I
Might conquer; or my ambition. Ah, but here
Both spur me on: my path is traced, — but where?
That's hid in the mist of time. I'll think upon't.
[*Exit.*

SCENE II. — *A Room, with a Banquet.*

[*A year has passed.*]

ISABELLA.

Time lags, and slights his duty. I remember
The days when he would fly. How sweet they were!
Then I rebuked his speed, and now — and now
I drench his wing with tears. How heavily
The minutes pass! Can he avoid me? No.
I hear a step come sounding through the hall.
It *is* the murderer, Sforza. Now, my heart!
Rise up in thy full strength, and do the act
Of justice bravely. So, he's here.

Enter SFORZA.

SFORZA.

My love!
O my delight, my deity! I am come
To thank you for being gracious. I am late?

ISABELLA.

No: in the best of times, sir.

SFORZA.

Yet you look
Not gay, my Isabella. Nought has happened
To shake your promise?

ISABELLA.

Be assured of that.
Doubt not, nor chide, my lord. My heart, you know,
Falls faint at times. To-night I'll do my best
To entertain you as you merit.

SFORZA.

Better, I hope, my Isabel.

ISABELLA.

Your grace
May challenge any thing; from me the most.
Although a widow, not divested quite
Of all her sorrows, I am here to smile
Like tearful April on you: but you'll grow
To vanity, sir, unless some stop be put
To your amorous conquests. I must do't.

SFORZA.

You shall,
You shall, my Isabella.

ISABELLA.

Sir, I will.

You shall be wholly mine, till — death shall part us.
I *have* been full of miseries: they have swelled
My heart to bursting. You shall soothe me.

SFORZA.

How?

ISABELLA.

We'll find a way: nay, not so free, my lord;
I must be won with words, (though hollow;) smiles,
And vows, (although you mean them not;) kind looks
And excellent flattery. Come, my lord, what say you?
I'm all impatience.

SFORZA.

Oh! what can I say?
Thou art so lovely, that all words must fail.
They of whom poets sing men say were shadows;
Thus will they swear of thee.

ISABELLA.

Alas! my lord,
I have no laureate here to lie in rhyme;
So must remain unsung.

SFORZA.

But *I* will have
Your name recorded in the sweetest verse;
And sculptors shall do honor to themselves

And their delicious art by fashioning thee;
And painters shall devise for us a story,
Where thou and I, love, shall be seen reclining,
Thou on my arm——

ISABELLA.

A happy thought!

SFORZA.

And in
The guise of the throned Juno; I as Jove,
In his diviner moments, languishing
Beneath thy look.

ISABELLA.

She was a shrew, my lord,
That queen o' the heavens, and I——

SFORZA.

Then thou shalt be drawn
Like her who, in old inimitable tales,
Was pictured gathering flowers in Sicily,
And raised to Pluto's throne: methinks she was
A beautiful prophecy of thee; and there
Mountains shall rise, and grassy valleys lie
Asleep i' the sun, and blue Sicilian streams
Shall wander, and green woods, (just touched with light,)
Shall yield their foreheads to some western wind,
And bend to bright Apollo as he comes

Smiling from out the east. What more? Why you
Shall kneel and pluck the flowers, and look aside
Hearkening for me; and — *I* will be there, (a god,)
Rushing tow'rds thee, my sweet Proserpina.

ISABELLA.

An ugly story!

SFORZA.

How, sweet?

ISABELLA.

You would take me
To — HELL then? but forgive me: I am ill;
Distract at times: we'll now forget it all.
Come, you will taste my poor repast?

SFORZA.

Oh, surely.

ISABELLA.

We'll be alone.

SFORZA.

'Tis better. Yet I have [*They feast.*
No relish for common viands. Shall I drink
To thee, my queen?

ISABELLA.

To me, sir. This (look on't)
Is a curious wine; and like those precious drops
Sought by philosophers, (the life elixir,)
Will make you immortal.

SFORZA.

Give it me, my love.
May you ne'er know an hour of sorrow.

ISABELLA.

Ha!
Stay, stay: soft, put it down.

SFORZA.

Why, how is this?

ISABELLA.

Would—would you drink without me? Shame upon you!
Look at this fruit: a sea-worn captain, one
Who had sailed all 'round the world, brought it for me
From the Indian isles; the natives there, men say,
Worship it. This.

SFORZA.

It has a luscious taste.
My nephew, when he lived, loved such a fruit.

ISABELLA.

Thanks, spirit of vengeance! [*Aside.*
Now you shall taste the immortal wine, my lord,
And drink a health to Cupid.

SFORZA.

Cupid, then.
He was a cunning god: he dimmed men's eyes,
'Tis prettily said i' the fable. But *my* eyes
(Yet how I love!) are clear as though I were
A stoic. Ah!

ISABELLA.

What ails my lord?

SFORZA.

The wine is cold.

ISABELLA.

You'll find it warmer, shortly.
It is its nature, as I'm told, to heat
The heart. My lord, I read but yesterday
Of an old man, a Grecian poet, who
Devoted all his life to wine, and died
O' the grape. Methinks 'twas just.

SFORZA

'Twas so. This wine——

ISABELLA.

And stories have been told of men whose lives
Were infamous, and so their end. I mean
That the red murderer has himself been murdered;
The traitor struck with treason: he who let
The orphan perish, came himself to want:
Thus justice and great God have ordered it!
So that the scene of evil has been turned
Against the actor; pain paid back with pain;
And—*poison given for poison.*

SFORZA.

Oh, my heart!

ISABELLA.

Is the wine still so cold, sir?

SFORZA.

I am burning.
Some water: I burn with thirst. Oh! what is this?

ISABELLA.

You're pale: I'll call for help. Here!

Servants *enter.*

ISABELLA.

Bind that man
To his seat.

SFORZA.

Ah! traitress.

ISABELLA.

Leave us now, — alone. [Servants *exeunt.*
My lord! I'll not deceive you: you have drank
Your last draught in this world.

SFORZA.

My heart, my heart!
Traitress! I faint — faint: ah!

ISABELLA.

I would have done
Some act of justice in a milder shape:
But it could not be. I felt that you must *die;*
For my sake, for my boy, for Milan. You
Murdered my lord husband. Stare not thus:
'Tis melancholy truth. You have usurped
The first place in the dukedom; have swept down
My child's rights to the dust. What say you, sir?
Do you impeach my story? While you've time,
Give answer. [*He dies.*
You are silent? then, are you
Condemned for ever. I could grieve, almost,
To see his ghastly stare. His eye is vague;
Is motionless. How like those shapes he grows,
That sit in stony whiteness over tombs,
Memorials of their cold inhabitants.

Speak! are you sunk to stone? What can you say
In your defence, sir? Turn your eyes away.
How dare you look at me, so steadily?
You shall be amorous no more. Must I
Rouse you? How idly his arms hang. Turn your eyes
Aside. I dare not touch him; yet I must.
Ha! he is dead — dead; slain by me! Great Heaven!
Forgive me; I'm a widow broken-hearted.
A mother too; 'twas for my child I struck.
Yon bloody man did press so hardly on us:
He would have torn my pretty bird from me:
I had but one: what could I do to save it?
There was no other way!

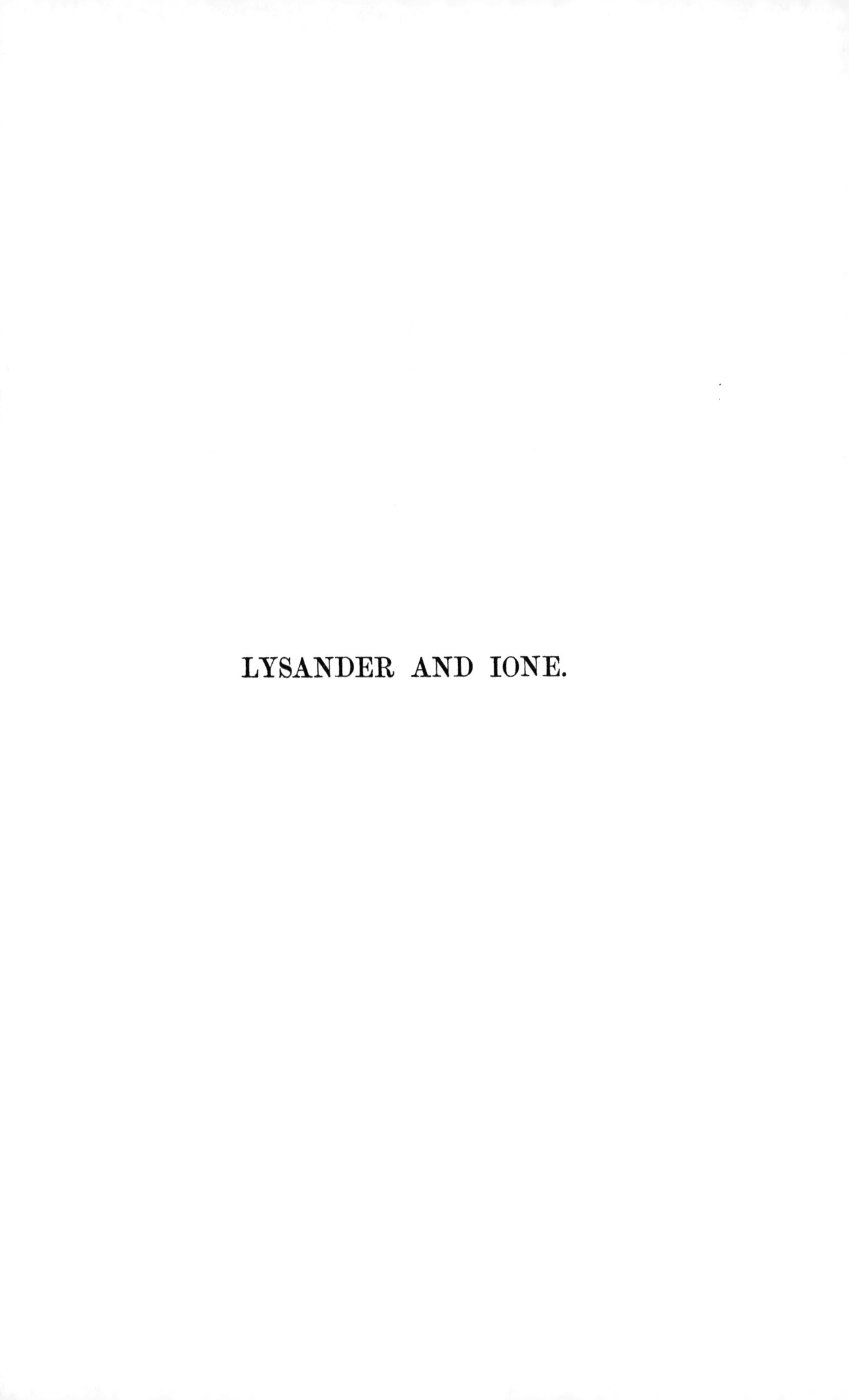

LYSANDER AND IONE.

Canst thou not tell me of a gentle pair? ——
Oh! if you have
Hid them in some flowery cave,
Tell me but where.

MILTON — *Comus.*

But she
Did not disdain to give his love contenting;
Cruel the soul that feeds on souls tormenting:
Nor did she scorn him, though not nobly born;
LOVE IS NOBILITY.

SPENSER — *Britain's Ida.*

LYSANDER AND IONE.

LYSANDER. IONE. (*A Wood.*)

LYSANDER.

Now, sit.

IONE.

Here?

LYSANDER.

Here:
The embroiderer, Moss, hath wrought you a golden seat.
Disdain her not, the yellow-tressed Moss;
For she is Nature's handmaid, decking aye
Her boddice with bright flowers; and when decay
Winters the rock or tree, her fringed gold
She leaves to hide the poor thing's poverty.

IONE.

So, there: now kneel and worship.

LYSANDER.

I will; I do: Oh! Heavens of love, I do.

Deep worshipper am I for one so young;
But Love has taught me: he matured my thought;
And so beyond my years I worship you.
Stay; stir not, sweet. Sit here.

IONE.

'Tis a fair place.

LYSANDER.

Ay; Iris hath been here, beloved one.
The rich Spring's almoner is she, who scatters
Upon the grateful world her sweets and flowers.
Bountiful Spring! Is it not strange that men
Will scorn or shun her favors? will bar out
The beauty of the day and vernal airs,
And die in dreams of freedom?

IONE.

You would talk
(And I might listen) till we both forgot,
That I have cares which call me.

LYSANDER.

We will meet
To-morrow early. I will show you all
The secrets of our forest. Every dell
And every leafy nook and cave o'ergrown,
The rock, the river, and the Dryad's oak
We'll see to-morrow. What, if we surprise
A wood-nymph sleeping?

IONE.

This to me?

LYSANDER.

Why, ay;
For then I'll show you how the true heart meets
Beauty unheeding.

IONE.

No, no.

LYSANDER.

You will come.
And I will be your guard, and servant, both;
And, as we pierce the untrodden woods, I'll teach
How you may shun the briery paths and pass
The snake untouched; and we will hear the songs —
Ha! do you smile? why then you'll come.

IONE.

No.

LYSANDER.

Yes.

IONE.

Be not too sure, Lysander. Foolish boy!
To give your heart to me, — to *me*, poor youth,
A spirit of the waters!

LYSANDER.

You are more;
My queen, my goddess! Sole and peerless queen!
And I your most true subject.

IONE.

I am one
Of old king Nereus' daughters, gentlest boy.
My home lies low beneath the eternal seas.
My country (tho' I sometimes earthward stray)
Is where the mariner's plummet never fell;
Down in the fathomless deep: the wild waves there
Sound not, nor dare the watery creatures come
To gaze upon those calm and sacred sands.
Beyond your reach my home is.

LYSANDER.

Pretty story!

IONE.

Believe it, fond Lysander, and forget me,
But, come; as you have loved me long and well,
Have you not sung my name to all the stars,
And vowed mine eyes were far more bright than they?
A lover? he should tell the skies his love,
And make the air acquainted with his woe;
Should tell to budding morn, to lazy noon,
To waters where the unsunned Dian comes

Dipping her silver feet, all his chaste joy.
But you *have* done this?

LYSANDER.

Often, oft.

IONE.

Indeed!
How did you name me?

LYSANDER.

Sweet Ione! Fair
And beautiful Ione! fair and dear!
Too dear, because too cold art thou to me.
Ione! list, — Ione! Pretty name!
Is it not yours?

IONE.

'Tis mine, and you shall sing
A forest song in its honor.

LYSANDER.

Listen, then, love; and with your white hand clear
Your marble forehead from its cloudy hair.
So, thus; your eye bent tow'rds me;
How brightly it burns upon me! Listen, sweet.
Yet, 'tis a melancholy song; confused;
Half dream and half despair. You will but smile at 't?

IONE.

Sing on, sing on: I love a wild song. Sing!

LYSANDER.

Now, by Night! I swear
I love thee, delicate Ione!
And, when I lean upon my thoughts at night,
My soul grows sick with love. In sleep, in dreams,
Thou, like a spirit from the haunted stars,
Stand'st plain before me. I have seen thee come
In pale and shadowy beauty to my side;
Or, floating 'tween me and the cloudless moon,
Stretch forth, like silver vapors, thy white arms,
And breathe upon my heart
Arabian odors, sweet, but cold as death.

I love thee; I have loved thée, long and well.
Ione, daughter of the eternal Sea;
Sea-born, but gifted with diviner life,
With human worth, and heavenly goodness crowned;
Peerless, perennial, without stain or taint,
Be mortal with immortal purity!

But thou art gone!
And now I wander when the gusty winds
Chase the dark clouds across the star-dropt plains:
For then methinks I see thee, pure and pale.
I love to lie by waterfalls, alone;

To hear the sad boughs moan,
When through the piny forest I pursue
My solitary way :
And then at times I dream, and *speak* to thee !
And thou, Ione, dost thou not (oh, say it !)
Bequeath soft messages for me,
Unto the dark boughs of the whispering pines ?

IONE.

Enough, enough. Your fancy grows too wild :
Reason must tame it, else some sharp reproof.
And so you love me ? Pshaw !

LYSANDER.

By all the gods !

IONE.

I'll not believe 't : what ! you ? so young a boy ?
'Twill be a pretty tale.

LYSANDER.

But who shall tell it ?

IONE.

Why I, and all who hear us ; for we are
Encompassed by the sylvan people here ;
And not a foolish hope hast thou confessed,
But Echo in her hundred caves has caught

The sound, and told it to the wood-nymphs' ears,
Whence, shaped like whispers from the forest boughs,
(All which, true traitors, shake while they betray
Poor human secrets,) thy mad words are borne
To the great Pan.

LYSANDER.

And he? Well, what of him?

IONE.

Oh! he loves all the nymphs who haunt his woods,
And when he finds they wander from their homes——

LYSANDER.

Fear him not; I am here, too, sweet Ione!

IONE.

My gentle boy! And so, you love me, — well?

LYSANDER.

Ay, like the stars.

IONE.

Not as a lover——

LYSANDER.

Oh!
I love you like the beauty of the world,
The rose, the——

IONE.

Peace, and hear me, young Lysander.
Some maids, high born as I am, in past times,
(Thus, if no fable, pale Œnone did)
Gave their great hearts to mortals. Mark what followed:
The men they graced forgot them.

LYSANDER.

Shall I swear?

IONE.

What have you done to win a Nereid's love?
Dost know, youth, that the princes of the sea;
Faunus, and many a wood-god; shapes that haunt
The groves and mountains and the running streams,
Have wooed me — *me* — in vain?

LYSANDER.

Oh, I believe it.
'Tis certain they have done 't; and I — even I
Have left my quiet home o' nights, to sing
Your soft sad name beside the noisy sea,
And hearken if in the watery tumult you
Whispered sweet answers. I have come hither, too,
At noon, at dusky eve, on darkest nights,
To seek you. I have let my unguarded sheep
Wander alone upon the mountains drear,
Have left my father (yet I love him well)
To weep my nightly absence; quitted all

Our village feasts and calm domestic meetings,
Here to resort and dream of the sweet Ione.

IONE.

Indeed, my love?

LYSANDER.

Again, — for dear love's sake!
For *my* sake; thus again.

IONE.

Why, then — my love!

LYSANDER.

Oh! my divine Ione! my heart's queen!
What shall I do to merit all this love?

IONE.

Be constant.

LYSANDER.

Ay, beyond fidelity.
I'll be more true
Than bright Apollo to the summer air,
Than larks to morn, or stars to cloudless eyes,
Or sweets to the maiden May. Oh! fear me not.

IONE.

I will not, dear Lysander. You and I

Will haunt these woods together: you shall pass
The busy morning hours amongst the hills,
And tend your father's flock; I in my cave
Beneath the seas must linger out the day;
But ever at night I'll meet you, dear Lysander,
And when stern fate shall lift you to the stars,
I from the salt sea wave will take my flight,
(Great Jove will not reject a sea-maid's prayer)
And dwell with you for ever. Now, farewell.

LYSANDER.

One kiss from that red rose which hides your lip!
One kiss? O love! how sweet; how all too sweet!

IONE.

Peace, peace! Farewell.

LYSANDER.

Until to-morrow morn!

IONE.

Until to-morrow only, then, farewell!

JUAN.

Like a village nurse
Stand I now cursing and considering, when
The tamest fool would do — I will be sudden,
And she shall know and feel, love in extremes
Abused, knows no degree of hate.

MASSINGER — *Duke of Milan.*

I come, Death! I obey thee,
Yet I will not die raging: for, alas!
My whole life was a frenzy. —
Bury me with Marcelia;
And let our epitaph be . . . .

The same.

JUAN.

SCENE — *The Gardens belonging to a Spanish Castle.*

JUAN *and a* BOY.

JUAN.

The night grows foul and dark ; and the thick air
Wakes pulses at my heart, which now should sleep.
Hark ! the winds draw the curtains of the sky,
Like ministers to lust. Queen Dian, now,
Is with her paramour.

BOY.

Spoke you, my lord ?

JUAN.

They'll rock her into slumber. She should watch ;
For others may be busy while she sleeps,
And stain her fame with falsehood. The hot air
Weighs on my forehead. Break a lemon branch
And give 't me, Lopez. So ; how fresh ! how cool !
(Tho' all its sweets are fled :) another — Thanks !
I'll bind them round my forehead. What time is 't ?

BOY.

Near midnight.

JUAN.

Wants it long?

BOY.

Some minutes; the last chimes have just now ceased.

JUAN.

They sounded sadly. Let me hear thee sing
A song; 'twill drive some blacker thoughts away.

BOY.

What sort of song? Shall it be tender? gay?

JUAN.

Let it be full of love, and foaming o'er;
But not a jot of kindness: burning passion;
No more: yes, headlong folly; flames that parch
And wither up the heart: fierce jealousy,
And horrid rage; and doubt and — dark despair!
Sing she you loved was false, and that you grew
Mad, and a murderer; anything.

BOY.

My lord!

JUAN.

Then you may say how she
Was beautiful as Sin, and that her eyes
Shone like the morning ; that her arms were smooth,
And gracefully turned, and that her figure seemed
Shaped from the mould of Dian's. You then may tell
How her white bosom rose and sank, at times,
To the music of her passionate heart. But, no ;
We'll have no music now ; my soul's untuned,
And discord is the only element.
A wife ? — When went my wife hence, boy ?

BOY.

Sir !

JUAN.

Where is your lady, fool ?

BOY.

At prayers, I think.

JUAN.

Excellent, excellent ! the times are good
(Must be) when strumpets pray. My bosom now
Swells like the boiling ocean. How *could* she
Be false to me ? to me who loved her more
Than heaven or hope hereafter. How I gazed
Upon her brow, and thought it fairer than

The face of the starry heavens! Begone, and send
Your mistress hither.

BOY.

She's at prayers, my lord.

JUAN.

Ha! true; forgot! no matter: leave me, sirrah,
And place the lamp upon the dial yonder,
But draw the shade around it. Now, go, go.

[Boy *goes out.*

Now then I am — alone. There's not a sound
To cheer my purpose: it is dark and close.
My sòul is dark; imprisoned in — a grave;
Yet, resolute to bear. Shall I revenge?
I'll kill her, tho' the stars dissolve in tears,
And thunder mutters help; and so, all's past.
Having resolved, the bloody part is done; —
And all the rest is mercy. She must perish.
I'll wash away her sins with all her blood.
Yet — if I slay her, I shall surely die.
Die? I am dead already; jealous hate,
Despair, and too much love have poisoned me.
Oh, widow, who hast lost thine all on earth,
What is thy pain to mine? A step? — a step?
She comes, then: not alone? ah! not alone.
Now for my hiding-place.

[*He retires.*

OLYMPIA *and* BIANCA *enter.*

OLYMPIA.

Did I believe in fables, I should think
Some evil hung about me: the black night
Has not allowed one small star to escape,
To light us on our path. Who's there? I thought
A figure passed us. Hark!

BIANCA.

I heard nothing.

OLYMPIA.

Nor I: and yet when dæmons walk about,
Their steps 'tis said are noiseless. I could now
Think half my nursery stories true, and spurn
My better reason from me.

BIANCA.

Let us talk
Of something else, dear lady.

OLYMPIA.

Tremble not.
You have no cause to fear; your days have been
Harmless, (I hope so,) and the spirits of ill
Leave innocent life untouched. Look, girl, the worm
Lights her green lamp; and, see! the fountain, there,
Into the night shoots up its silver rain.

How fresh and sweet it is! how musical.
Bianca, get you homewards; I will rest
Here, in the cool awhile. [BIANCA *exit.*
What a most delicate air this garden hath!
There's scarce a flower or odorous shrub that lives
We have not. There, how clearly I scent the rose;
And now the limes; and now, as the sad wind
Sobs, an uncertain sweetness comes from out
The orange-trees. Their fragrance charms me
Almost to sleep.

[*Reclines.*

JUAN *enters.*

JUAN.

She sleeps at last, then: yet I will not kill
The frail thing sleeping. Why did I delay?
I feared (why did I fear?) to meet her eye;
The eye of her whom justice bids me strike?
Oh! what a beautiful piece of sin is there!
They fabled well who said that woman won
Man to perdition. Hark! the thunder mutters;
And lightnings. Rest, wild spirits, I am come
To save ye a worthless task. Now then, my soul!
Rise up, Olympia! (she sleeps soundly.) Ho!
Stirring at last. Rise, Fair Olympia: you
Have much to do to-night. The fates have writ
Your early doom upon their brazen book;
And I must do their bidding.

OLYMPIA.

What is this?

JUAN.

Now by — but I am quiet. You have sinned
Most foully 'gainst your husband : that's not much;
But you have done a deed at which the skies
Blacken. Look up.

OLYMPIA.

Dear Juan?

JUAN.

You have made
Me (I forgive that) base : our noble house,
'Till now illustrious, you have stained. Hark, hark!
The voices that you hear amongst the clouds
(But understand not) say 'confess your sin.'
I wait to hear it.

OLYMPIA.

Oh, your mind is filled
With dreaming terrors. Let us home, dear Juan;
We'll talk to-morrow of this.

JUAN.

Talk? to-morrow?
Now, by the burning passion that doth stir
Vengeance within me, Olympia! This night

You take your leave of earth. Yet, ere you die,
I'll tell you how I loved you ; doated — oh !
Grew guilty for you : guilty, do you hear ?

OLYMPIA.

Most perfect, sir ; I tremble.

JUAN.

Ere you married
I loved you ; that you know : your father shook
A poor petitioner away ; and you
(Although you owned to love) forsook me. Then
I tried my fortune in the wars : you gave
Your hand to old Ramirez.

OLYMPIA.

I was bid.

JUAN.

My uncle's death raised me to wealth, and then
I came home quickly : you were married.

OLYMPIA.

Well !

JUAN.

Well !
Why then despair possessed me. Madness stamped
His brand upon my brain, and years flamed on,

(You still Ramirez' wife,) when I became
A man again. The impudent dotard laughed,
Boasting he had out-schemed a younger man,
Me,—*me.* My curse upon him!

OLYMPIA.

Peace; no more.

JUAN.

So, you still love him?

OLYMPIA.

Sir, I love him not.
But I disdain the madman that belies him.

JUAN.

Mad? mad? Now shall you die,—*die!* (do you hear?)
By me, who love you. Mad? *I have* been mad;
But 'twas because I lost you; you, thrice false one!
Now, being sane, 't shall be my bloody care
To see none rave like me from too much love.
Mad? mad? and *you* to jeer me? Blighting shame
Weigh on your soul for that.

OLYMPIA.

You have belied
My husband's honored name.

JUAN.

His name?
I slew him, harlot! stabbed him thro' and thro'.
Ha, ha, ha, ha! Thou fool, who couldst believe
That common villains struck and robbed him not.

OLYMPIA.

I dream; I hope I dream.

JUAN.

'Twas I. Laugh out!
Yet if thou dost 'twill be at my great woe.
And though thou jeerest me, I deserve it not.
For all was done for thee; and now hast thou
Called back the love I bought at such a price,
And sold it to another.

OLYMPIA.

Sir, 'tis false:
You are all false. How I abhor you now!
Hearken, Don Juan; I have loved you, (how
You will remember quickly;) 'twas an error:
For had I known his blood was spilt by you,
I would have cast you off, as now I do,
For ever.

JUAN.

Speak again.

OLYMPIA.

For ever ; ever.

JUAN.

Will — will your paramour come then ? Ha, ha, ha !
He waits, and wishes. Do not keep him long.

OLYMPIA (*aside*).

God ! he is mad, indeed. I must escape.

JUAN.

Stay ! Stop ! but weep not ; pray not : wouldst thou pray
To the deaf adder ? to the insensate sea ?
Look, I am stern, but just ; determined, wronged ;
A judge, and you the victim.

OLYMPIA.

Let me pass.

JUAN.

Kneel down before the gods. Now answer me.
Lovest thou, or not, (speak truly, for thou speak'st
Thy last words to the world,) this stranger ? Quick !

OLYMPIA.

I love him. (JUAN *cries out.*) But ——

JUAN.

Traitress ! adultress !
I strike (*stabs her*) — and kill my wrongs !

OLYMPIA.

Stay, Juan, stay! but no; 'tis past — and over.
It cannot be: — you've done ill.

JUAN.

You — you are
Not hurt? not slain? Speak!

OLYMPIA.

Save yourself, dear Juan.
That youth ——

JUAN.

Yes, yes.

OLYMPIA.

He is my brother.

JUAN.

Hell!

OLYMPIA.

The Inquisition now are watching for him.
Save him.

JUAN.

I will.

OLYMPIA.

By — ah ——

[*Dies.*

JUAN.

By my lost soul.
Look up, look up, Olympia! Juan's here;
Thy husband, — murderer, (that's the name:) My love!
My love! Olympia! I — she's dead. [*A pause.*
How's this?
So, where am I? Olympia! she is false.
Dead? Ah! some villain has been busy here.
By heaven, the golden hair is wet: the eye
Has lost its tender meaning. Life and love
Have fled together — to the grave. Was 't I?
Oh! I have cut those sweet blue veins asunder,
And filled her breast with blood. There's not a touch
Of color in her lip, (so red once,) and her hand
Falls: it will never press my own again.
What a voice she had! 'tis silent! Could it die
In a single groan? Impossible.

(*Voices are heard.*)

My lord!

JUAN.

Hark, hark! they call the murderer. He is here.

(*Voices.*

My lord, my lord!

JUAN.

Now, first to hide

The body. *Body!*—is she changed so soon?
[*Hides the body.*
And now to fly; yet wherefore? Can they read
In my white visage and unaltered eye
A murder redder than the crime of Cain?
I'll stay and dream of death. Oh! I have lost
What was my life on earth; what *was*, alas!
A horrid sound. They come. [*Enter* Servants.
Whom seek ye? She—
Your lady's gone; gone, do you doubt me? Gone.

SERVANT.

My lord! a stranger has arrived; her brother.

JUAN

Who? what? She has none; none.

SERVANT.

My lord, he's at the castle.

JUAN.

Peace! She is gone
On a dark journey. Oh!

SERVANT.

You've cut your hand, sir.

JUAN.

I have cut—my heart.
Leave me; all but Diego. [Servants *go out.*

Poor old man,
You were my father's servant; nay *his* father's.
We prized you, and you served us faithfully;
But now's your service ended. Old Diego!
Long before sunrise I shall be ——

DIEGO.

My lord!

JUAN.

Quiet, Diego. No foul passions, then,
No turbulent love, nor fierce idolatry,
Nor bitter hate, nor jealousy, shall mar
My solitary rest. I shall be — dead.
The last ('tis pity) of a princely house;
Let not our name be slandered.

DIEGO.

My dear lord!

JUAN.

One old man thought
I should do honor to his name; — that's past;
For look! my star is setting. I am now
The last of a famous line, which backward ran
To the blood of kings, and then was lost in time.
Ah! where is now my father's prophecy,
And where my own hopes? Withered, withered.

DIEGO.

Alas!

JUAN.

A few more words, and then — and then, good night.
I smote — I smote — now let the black skies fall
And crush me in a moment. Oh! my queen!
My own incomparable wife! My love!
Oh! all my life has been an error. So,
I'll shift a troublesome burden from my back,
And lay me down to sleep.

DIEGO.

Beseech you, home!

JUAN.

We'll do as thou dost say. That rich red draught,
Which filled the frames of aged men with youth,
And strung their sinews like the bracing air,
Were now an useless medicine.

DIEGO.

Noble master!
Let me for once forget my place, dear lord!
And bid you hope for comfort.

JUAN.

Hush, hush, hush!
No more a lord: a vulgar slave am I,

Who caught one look from heaven; but the soft light
Is out, which was my guide; and here I stand
Lost, and in terrible darkness near my tomb.
And angry shadows beckon me; fierce shapes
And fears (which no hope tempers) drag me on.
Look, I must go: yet first we'll make all plain,
And leave the earth a warning. I —— the story
Hangs on my tonguè. I smote — I — look aside
While I burst forth in guilt. I smote — Oh God!
The tenderest, noblest woman in the world;
And with my cruel dagger cut a road
To a heart where I was lord; but knew it not.
Ay, weep, Diego; thou may'st weep, poor man;
But for myself my tears are dried to dust:
Burnt and scorched up by pain. But let's be still.
Your hand, my last firm friend; I have not yet
Forgotten how you used (bright years ago)
To bear me, then a boy, sport-tired, home.
Bear me so far once more: 'tis your last toil;
And lay me gently on my marble bed,
And ask no man to curse me! All's done. Now
Open your arms, Olympia!

[*Stabs himself.*

THE WAY TO CONQUER.

Hamlet. I have heard
That guilty creatures sitting at a play
Have, by the very cunning of the scene,
Been struck so to the soul, that presently
They have proclaimed their malefactions.

Hamlet.

Lov. He gave him first his breeding;
Then showered his bounties on him like the Hours,
That, open-handed, sit upon the clouds,
And press the liberality of Heaven
Down to the laps of thankful men.

BEN JONSON — *New Inn.*

THE WAY TO CONQUER.

[A story distantly resembling this sketch is told of one of the Dukes of Guise.]

SCENE—*A Room in a Palace.*

PRINCE. CESARIO.

CESARIO.

Your highness sent for me?

PRINCE.

I did: sit down.
You look ill, dear Cesario?

CESARIO.

No, my lord.

PRINCE.

You have been feasting lately? Yes, 'tis so:
You were at Count Vitelli's banqueting.
But have a care, it is not good for health.

CESARIO.

You sent for me
In haste, was it not so?

PRINCE.

Not so.

CESARIO.

Then shall I come to-morrow?

PRINCE.

Let it be
To-day, now you are here. Cesario!
Is there not one who lives with old Colonna?
A foreign youth? Dost know him?

CESARIO.

Ay, my lord,
'Tis Pedro — no, Diego, — a dark Spaniard;
A linguist, learned, and noble; a cadet
Of the great house of — of Medina, sir.

PRINCE.

You know him well?

CESARIO.

I know him; yet not well.

PRINCE.

Should'st think him honest?

CESARIO.

Honest, sir? Oh, surely.

PRINCE.

Then he'd not betray
Your uncle, as I hear he has done?

CESARIO.

Sir! He?
He could not be so base: my uncle was
His first and excellent friend.

PRINCE.

I thought the world
Was not so bad. Now listen, Cesario,
And you shall hear a curious history.
Keep Diego in your mind the while, and think
That he's the hero of it. Last night a man
Came mask'd unto a rich lord's house, (here in
Palermo;) — Do you hear how Etna mutters?

CESARIO.

It sends a terrible sound indeed, my lord.

PRINCE.

This man petitioned for his life. He said
That he had sworn to act a horrid deed,
And came to make disclosure. The great lord

(His was the life in danger) promised full
Forgiveness : — but you do not hear my words ?

CESARIO.

Pardon me, sir, I hear.

PRINCE.

The culprit said
A youth on whom this lord had lavished wealth,
And kindness and good precept, had forgot
His better tutoring, and lent deaf ears
To those divinest whispers which the soul
Breathes to prevent our erring. He resolved
To kill his benefactor : that was bad.

CESARIO.

Oh ! he deserved ——

PRINCE.

We'll talk of that hereafter.
Well, this bad man whose mind was spotted thus —
Was leprosied by foul ingratitude,
Had sworn to murder this his friend.

CESARIO.

My lord !

PRINCE.

I see it pains you : yes, for the sake of gold,

He would have slain his old and faithful friend;
Have spurned the few gray locks that time had left,
And stopped the current of his reverend blood,
Which *could* not flow much longer.

CESARIO.

Are you sure?

PRINCE.

The plan was this: they were to bind him fast,
(To slay him here were dangerous,) and transport
His body to some lonely place.

CESARIO.

What — place?

PRINCE.

I'll tell you, for I once
Was housed there through a storm. A castle stands
Fronting Calabria, on the rough sea-coast.
A murder once was done there, and e'er since
It has been desolate; 'tis bleak, and stands
High on a rock, whose base was caverned out
By the wild seas ages ago. The winds
Moan and make music through its halls, and there
The mountain-loving eagle builds his home.
But all's a waste: for miles and miles around
There's not a dwelling.

CESARIO.

Is 't near the — eastward foot
Of Etna, — where Muralto's villa stands?

PRINCE.

Yes, yes; well guessed: I see you know the spot.
Now, dear Cesario, could'st thou think a man,
Setting aside all ties, could do a deed
Of blackness there? Why, 'tis within the reach
Of Etna, and some thirty years ago,
(The last eruption,) when the lava rivers
Went flaming toward that point, this dwelling stood
In danger. I myself stood near the place,
And saw the bright fires stream along, when they
Crumbled the chestnut forests and dark pines
And branching oaks to dust. The thunder spoke,
The rebel waves stood up and lashed the rocks,
And poured their stormy cries through every cave.
Each element rose in riot: the parched earth
Staggered and spouted fire ——

CESARIO.

Oh! sir, no more.

PRINCE.

Fancy, Cesario, in this desolate house,
How ghastly the poor murdered wretch would look;
His hanging head, and useless neck; his old
Affectionate heart that beat so fondly, now

Like a stilled instrument. I could not kill
A dog that loved me: could you?

CESARIO.

No, sir — no.

PRINCE.

Why, how you tremble!

CESARIO.

'Tis a fearful picture.

PRINCE.

Yet might it have been true.

CESARIO.

We'll hope not.

PRINCE.

Hope!
That hope is past. How will the Spaniard look,
Think you, Cesario, when the question comes
Home to his heart? In truth he could not look
More pale than you are now. Cesario!
The eye of God has been upon him.

CESARIO.

Yes:
I hope ——

PRINCE.

Beware.

CESARIO.

My lord!

PRINCE.

Beware, how you
Curse him; for he is loaded heavily.
Sin and fierce wishes plague him, and the world
Will stamp its malediction on his head,
And God and man disown him.

CESARIO.

Oh! no more.
No more, my dearest lord; behold me here,
Here at your feet, a wretch indeed, but now
Won quite from crime. Spare me.

PRINCE.

Rise. I forgive
The ingratitude to me: but men like you
(Base, common, *bribed* stabbers) must not roam
About the world so freely.

CESARIO.

Oh! that now
You could but see my heart.

PRINCE.

I would not see
Your bosom's base and black inhabitant.
Now listen to me again: speak not, but listen.
This is a different tale. Cesario!
When first you came to Sicily, you were
A little child: your noble father, worn
By toil and long misfortune, scarce had time
To beg protection for you ere he died.
Since then, if in your memory I have failed
In kindness tow'rd you, or good counselling,
Reproach me.

CESARIÒ.

You have been most kind; too kind.

PRINCE.

Once, 'twas in terrible sickness, when none else
Would tread your infectious chamber, (think on that,)
I, though your prince ——

CESARIO.

In pity!

PRINCE.

Hear me speak.
I gave that healing medicine to your lips,
Which wanting you had died. I tended you:
And was your nurse through many a sultry night;
For you were quite abandoned ——

CESARIO.

Quite, quite, quite.

PRINCE.

Time passed, and you recovered, and could use
Your sword again: you tried it 'gainst my blood,
(My nephew then,) and I forgave it.

CESARIO.

That
Was in the heat of quarrel.

PRINCE.

I have said
That I forgave it. Then a most mean wish
(You wished my wealth) possessed you. I could never,
I own it, have guessed at that.

CESARIO.

Oh! sir, not so.

PRINCE.

Well, then, it was not: but Aurelia's charms
(That cunning Phryne) have o'erwhelmed your sense;
All gratitude and good being gone.

CESARIO.

My lord!
My father! oh, once more believe me. I

Do not deserve you should: but if you can
Once again credit me, may hell's fierce torments —
But, no; I will not pain or shame your love:
Nay more, I will deserve it. I can die
Now, for my mind has grown within this hour
To firmness: yet, I now could wish to live,
To show you what I am.

PRINCE.

Cesario! hear me.
Hear and forget not — what your old friend says.
The world will blame me, but I'll try you still:
You cannot have the heart (I know you have one)
Again to harm me. Once, imperial Cæsar
Upon the young deluded Cinna laid
His absolute pardon: 'twas a weight that he
Could ne'er shake off. Cesario, thus
From my soul I now forgive you.

CESARIO.

Thanks.

PRINCE.

What, ho!
Cesario, faint not. Why, thou'rt weaker now
Than when Aurelia kissed your lip, and won
Your soul to sin. Come: — nay, there's no one knows
Our quarrel. Let us bury it in our breasts,
And talk as we were wont.

CESARIO.

A little time,
My lord, and I may thank you. Now, if I
Might dare to ask it, I would fain retire,
And dwell on all your goodness.

PRINCE.

Farewell, then.

CESARIO.

My noble prince, rest soundly: you have gained
Cesario's soul twice over. If a knave
Should say I wrong you now, believe him not.
If I myself should swear I was your foe,
Discredit me. Oh! once more on my knees,
I thank you: dearest father! look upon
Your prodigal son. Thanks — from my heart.

PRINCE.

Farewell,
Farewell, Cesario. Nay, compose yourself.
Now go. Farewell, farewell.

THE BROKEN HEART.

Pistol. Thou hast spoke the right ;
His heart is fracted and corroborate.

Henry V.

THE BROKEN HEART.

[This sketch is founded upon a tale of Boccaccio. The story is this: — Jeronymo was sent from Italy to Paris, in order to complete his studies. He was detained there two years, his mother being fearful lest he should marry a poor and beautiful girl (Sylvestra), with whom he had been brought up from his infancy. During his absence, his mother contrived to have Sylvestra married. He returned, and, after wandering about her dwelling, succeeded in getting into her chamber, conversed with her (her husband being asleep), and, at last, died on the bed before her.]

SCENE I. — *A Room.*

Jeronymo. His Mother.

MOTHER.

What have I said that you affect this humor?
Come, look less strangely. Is your anger dumb?
Speak out. Jeronymo?

JERONYMO.

You have done this?

MOTHER.

I did. 'Twas for your good.

JERONYMO.

Oh, mother, mother!
You have broke the fondest heart in Italy.
My good, what's that? Is't good that I shall die?
Is't good that I shall pine and fade away,
And take no comfort? None? O yes! Through all
My melancholy days I'll haunt the nest
Where my white dove lies guarded ——

MOTHER.

Patience, boy.

JERONYMO.

Until I die, stern mother. I shall die,
Like people smit by lightning, suddenly.

MOTHER.

Live and be crowned with Love.

JERONYMO.

Why so I will,
And wear white roses on my ghastly brow,
And laugh at fate, like that forced bride who fell
Dead on her marriage morning. I'll be gone.
If she be false — Come with me, madam! False?
Sylvestra false? Sylvestra?

MOTHER.

Name her not,

The bitter cause whence all our sorrow springs.
You must not think of her.

JERONYMO.

Not think of her?

MOTHER.

No; she is married.

JERONYMO.

Ha, ha, ha! good mother.
Shame on your cruel jest: be grave — and gentle.

MOTHER.

I told you this before: she's married — married!
Do I speak plain.

JERONYMO.

Too plain, if you speak true.
That you may know I heed your tale, look at me!
Am I not — broken-hearted?

MOTHER.

Oh! sweet heavens.
I have done too much. (*Aside*) How pinched and pale he looks!
Jeronymo, my child!

JERONYMO.

Your only child.

MOTHER.

Why do you talk thus? Prythee think on me;
On me, your mother.

JERONYMO.

Surely; for you thought
Of me in absence. I've a grateful soul:
I'll make you heir of all my father's lands,
His gems, and gold, and floating argosies:
All shall be yours; I will not live to leave
Widow or child to rob so kind a mother.

MOTHER.

Peace, peace, you hurt my heart.

JERONYMO.

I swear to do't.
By those dark Three who cut the threads of life!
By Plutus, God of gold! By Minos, judge,
And cruel Cupid! By my own lost life,
And murdered hopes, I swear!

MOTHER.

Oh! Do not talk thus.
If not for me, yet for your father's sake,
Spare me, my son!

JERONYMO.

My father? He is dead.

MOTHER.

But when he lived he was most merciful;
Tempering the angry feelings which will rise
In every mind (and lead in some to ruin)
By draughts of that divine philosophy——

JERONYMO.

O, the brave drink! Abroad, abroad, we had
Huge flasks which all went flaming to the brain.
Dark, sweet, and full of sin; and so I drank,
And drank, and drank the livelong day and night,
And chewed the bitter laurel for my food,
Whose roots are watered, as wild poets tell,
By the immortal wells of Castaly.

MOTHER.

Alas, alas!

JERONYMO.

Why that looks well. I love it.

MOTHER.

What do you love, my son?

JERONYMO.

To see you weep,
Although your husband died so long ago.

MOTHER.

I do not weep for him.

JERONYMO.

Not weep for him?
Then shame seal up your mouth. Was he not kind?
Was he not good? He was; and yet you weep not:
Weep you the lazy lonely widow's life?
Tush! you may buy another husband yet.

MOTHER.

I do not wish 't. I cannot match the last.

JERONYMO.

You cannot, madam; (that was true at least.)
No, though you gaze from evening dusk, till Morn
Comes climbing up the bright steps of the East;
Nay, tho' you watch for hearts from dawn till dark.
Unmatchable 'mongst men, so kind, so true,
Abhorring falsehood with a natural hate,
And full of pity was he,—but he died;
Good father! how he loved his poor pale son,
And how he feared (do you remember that?)
His race should end with me. He wished—vain wishes!
No child of mine shall ever bear our name,
And make 't more noble. Lo, I am the last!
The last, last scion of a gracious tree;
For you, my mother, now have struck me down,
And withered all my branches. So, farewell.
[*Going.*

MOTHER.

Farewell! Yet stay! Leave pardon with me. Stay!

JERONYMO.

Farewell, and pardon! Blessings (if the son
May bless the mother) rest upon your heart.
Be calm, be happy. Think of me no more.

SCENE II. — *Sylvestra's Chamber.*

JERONYMO. SYLVESTRA.

JERONYMO.

So, all is hushed at last. Hist! There she lies,
Who *should* have been my own. Sylvestra! Hark!
She sleeps! and from her parted lips there comes
A fragrance, such as April mornings steal
From awakening flowers. There lies her arm, (sweet
arm!)
More white than marble, on the quilted lid.
'Tis motionless. What if she lives not? Oh!
How beautiful she is! How far beyond
Those bright creations, which the fabling Greeks
Placed on their cold Olympus. That great queen
Before whose eye Jove's starry armies shrank
To darkness, and the wide and billowy seas
Grew calm, was a leper to her. Look, oh, look!
Her beauty (that most pure divinity)
Doth sway the troubled blood till it stands charmed,
Adoring. — Hark, she murmurs. Oh, how soft!
Sylvestra!

SYLVESTRA.

Ha! who's there?

JERONYMO.

'Tis I.

SYLVESTRA.

Who is it ?

JERONYMO.

Must I then speak, and tell my name to you ?
Sylvestra ! know me now : not now ? O Pain !
Hath grief indeed so changed my voice ; so much
That you — *you* know me not ? Alas !

SYLVESTRA.

Begone !
I'll wake my husband if you move a step.

JERONYMO.

Jeronymo, Jeronymo ! 'tis I.

SYLVESTRA.

Ha ! speak again : yet, no, no ——

JERONYMO.

Hide your eyes :
Ay, hide them, married woman ! lest they look
On the wreck of him who loved you.

SYLVESTRA.

Loved me ? No.

JERONYMO.

Loved you like life, like heaven and happiness ;
Loved you, and wore your image on his heart
(Ill boding amulet) 'till death.

SYLVESTRA.

Alas !

JERONYMO.

And now I come to bring your wandering thoughts
Back to their innocent home. Do you not know,
Pale spirits have left their leaden urns, to tempt
Wretches from sin ? Some have been heard to laugh
Ghastlily on — the bed of wantonness,
And touch the limbs with death.

SYLVESTRA.

You will not harm me ?

JERONYMO.

Why not ? — No, no, poor girl ! I would not mar
Your delicate limbs with outrage. I have loved
Too well for that ; too long ; all our short lives.

SYLVESTRA.

Our sad short lives !

JERONYMO.

Sylvestra, you and I

Were children here some few short springs ago,
And loved like children : I the elder ; you
The loveliest girl that ever tied her hair
Across a sunny brow of Italy.
I still remember how, though others wooed,
You ever preferred me.

SYLVESTRA.

I did, I did.

JERONYMO.

I think you loved me. How I loved, my heart
Still tells me trembling. So I fain would bring
You comfort ere I go. Speak! the time's short,
For death has touched me.

SYLVESTRA.

You are jesting now?

JERONYMO.

Sweet, I am dying — dying. All my blood
Grows colder as I talk ; my pulses strike
More slowly ; and before the morning sun
Visits your chamber through those trailing vines,
I shall lie here — here in your chamber — dead.

SYLVESTRA.

You fright me.

JERONYMO.

Yet I'd not do so, Sylvestra.

I will but tell you, you have used me harshly,
(That is not much,) and die : nay, fear me not.
I would not chill, with this decaying touch,
That bosom where the blue veins wander 'round,
Nor should thy cheek, still fresh in beauty, fade
From fear of *me*, a poor heart-broken wretch !
Look at me. Why, the winds sing through my bones,
And children jeer me, and the boughs that wave
And whisper loosely in the summer air,
Shake their green leaves in mockery, as to say,
" We are the longer livers."

SYLVESTRA.

Kill me not.

JERONYMO.

I've numbered eighteen winters. Much may lie
In that short compass ; but *my* days have been
Not happy. Death was busy with our house
Early, and nipped the comforts of my home,
And sickness paled my cheek, and fancies (wild,
Strange, bright, delusive stars) came wandering by me.
There's one you know of : that — no matter — that
Drew me from out my way, (a perilous guide,)
And left me sinking. I had gay hopes too,
But heed them not ; they are vanished.

SYLVESTRA.

I — Oh, heart !

I thought, (speak softly, for my husband sleeps,)
I thought, when you did stay abroad so long,
And never sent nor asked of me or mine,
You'd quite forgotten Italy.

JERONYMO.

Speak again.
Was't so, indeed?

SYLVESTRA.

Indeed, indeed.

JERONYMO.

I see it;
The mother's pride, the woman's treachery.
Yet, what had I done Fortune that she could
Abandon me so entirely? Never mind 't:
Have a good heart, Sylvestra: they who hate
Can kill us, but no more; that's comfort, dear!
We'll fly from our pursuers, and be quiet.
The journey is but short, and we can reckon
On slumbering sweetly with the freshest earth
Sprinkled about us. There no storms can shake
Our secure tenement; nor need we fear,
Though cruelty be busy with our fortunes,
Or scandal with our names.

SYLVESTRA.

Alas, alas!

JERONYMO.

Sweet! in the land to come we'll feed on flowers.
Droop not, my child. A happy place there is:
Know you it not? (all pain and wrong shut out)
Where man may mix with angels. You and I
Will wander there with garlands on our brows,
And talk in music. We will shed no tears,
Save those of joy; nor sighs, unless for love.
Look up and straight grow happy. We may love
There without fear: no mothers there, no gold,
Nor hate, nor human perfidy; none, none.
Sweet one, we have been wronged. My own delight!
Too late I see thy gentle constancy:
Too late thy unstained love. Did'st think me changed?
Why I wrote, and wrote long, fond letters; all,
Steeped all in tears; I wrote, but you were silent.
At last suspicion touched me. I came home;
And found you married.

SYLVESTRA.

Alas!

JERONYMO.

Then I — Then I
Grew moody, and at times I fear my brain
Was fevered; but I could not die, Sylvestra,
And bid you no farewell.

SYLVESTRA.

Jeronymo!

Break not my heart thus; they — I was betrayed.
They told me you had found a face more fair
Than poor Sylvestra's; that (grown false) you had learned
To scorn your poor and childish love; ah, me!
They threatened, swore your heart was breaking; yes,
Because it wanted freedom. Then — look aside —
Then — then they — married me.

JERONYMO.

Oh! [*Cries out.*

SYLVESTRA.

What is't? Speak!

JERONYMO.

The melancholy winds, which shun the day,
And mourn abroad at dark, are chanting now
A funeral dirge for me. Sweet, let me lie
Once on thy breast: I will not chill 't, my love,
With my cold cheek; nor stain it with a tear.
It is a shrine where innocent love might lie;
Where murdered love should end. For once, Sylvestra?

SYLVESTRA.

Pity me!

JERONYMO.

How I pity!

SYLVESTRA.

Talk not thus;
Though you but jest, it makes me tremble.

JERONYMO.

Jest?
Look in my eyes, and mark how true my story.
Nay look: for on their glassy surface lies
Death, my Sylvestra. It is Nature's last
And beautiful effort, to bequeath a fire
To orbs whereon the Spirit sate thro' life,
And looked out in its moods of thought and joy,
Revealing all that inward worth and power,
Which else would want their true interpreters.

SYLVESTRA.

Why, now you're cheerful.

JERONYMO.

Yes; 'tis thus I'd die.

SYLVESTRA.

Now *I* must smile.

JERONYMO.

Do so, and I'll smile too.
I do; albeit — ah! now my parting words
Lie heavy on my tongue; my lips obey not;
And — speech — comes difficult from me. While I can,
Farewell. Your hand! I cannot see it.

SYLVESTRA.

Ah! — cold.

JERONYMO.

'Tis so: but scorn it not, my own poor girl.
They've used us hardly — hardly; yet thou wilt
Forgive them? One's a mother, and may feel,
When that she knows me dead. Some air; more air:
Where are you? I am blind; my hands are numbed:
This is a wintry night. So, — cover me.

[*Dies.*

THE FALCON.

"Frederigo, of the Alberighi family, loved a gentlewoman, and was not requited with like love again. But, by bountiful expenses and over-liberal invitations, he wasted all his lands and goods, having nothing left him but a hawk or faulcon. His unkind mistress happened to come to visit him, and he not having any other food for her dinner, made a dainty dish of his faulcon for her to feed on. Being conquered by this exceeding kind courtesie, she changed her former hatred towards him, accepting him as her husband in marriage, and made him a man of wealthy possessions." — *Boccaccio*. (Old translation.) Fifth day: Novel 9.

THE FALCON.

SCENE I.— *Outside of a Cottage. Sunset.*

FREDERIGO (*alone*).

Oh! Poverty, and have I learnt at last
Thy bitter lesson? Thou forbidding power
That hast such sway upon this thriving earth,
Stern foe to comfort, sleep's disquieter;
What have I done that thou should'st smite me thus?
An open hand had I in happier times,
And when the feathered Fortune bore me high,
I scattered gifts below.
. . . . . . 'Tis the set of Sun!
How like a hero who hath run his course
In glory doth he die! His parting look
(Too beautiful for death) lights up the west
With crimson, and deep dyes the wandering clouds
With every tint that makes the rainbow fair.
Bright King! not unattended dost thou leave
The world that loved thee. Earth, and all her crowds,
Which late were joyous, pay dumb homage now;
Unutterable stillness, golden calm,
The winds and waves unmoving.

Sometimes one lonely note is heard, which marks
And makes more rich the silence; nothing more!
Thus, in great cities, the cathedral clock,
Lifting its iron tongue, doth seem to stay
Time for a moment, while it warns the world,
(Sweet sound to those who wake, or watch till morn,)
"Now goes the midnight." Then I love to walk
And hear that hoarse slow-fading clang grow sweet,
As upwards to the stars and mighty moon
It bears calm tidings from this dreaming globe.
Ah! why may not the poor man ever dream!
A step? Who's there? A lady? O, Giana!

GIANA *and her* MAID *enter.*

GIANA.

You have cause to be surprised, sir.

FREDERIGO.

No, dear lady;
Honored I own, that my poor dwelling should
Receive so fair a guest.

GIANA.

You have forgotten
The past times then?

FREDERIGO.

No, no; those sweet times live,
Flowers in my faithful memory, kept apart

For holier hours, and sheltered from the gaze
Of rude uncivil strangers; they are now
My only comfort; so lest they should fade
I use 'em gently, very gently, madam,
And water 'em all with tears.

GIANA.

Your poverty
Has made you gloomy, Signior Frederigo.

FREDERIGO.

Pardon me, madam: 'twas not well, indeed,
To meet such a guest with sorrow: you were born
For happiness.

GIANA.

Alas! I fear not so.

FREDERIGO.

Oh! yes, yes: and you well become it; well.
May grief ne'er trouble you, nor heavier hours
Weigh on so light a heart.

GIANA.

You well reprove me;
Light and unfeeling.

FREDERIGO.

Yet I meant not so.
Giana! let me sink beneath your scorn

If ever I reproach you : what am I,
Outcast from Fortune, all my father's gifts
Lavished and lost by folly——

GIANA.

'Twas for me.

FREDERIGO.

Oh! no, no : I had many faults
Whose burthen rests with me : then what am I,
That I should dare reproach you? As I am,
Know me your truest servant; only that;
And bound to live and die for you.

GIANA.

No more.
Let us enjoy the present.

MAID.

My lady, sir,
Is come to feast with you.

GIANA.

'Tis even so.

FREDERIGO.

I am too honored. Can you then put up
With my (so poor a) welcoming? If the heart
Could spend its wealth in entertainment, I

Would feast you like a queen: but, as it is,
You will interpret kindly?

GIANA.

Oh! I know
I come to a scholar's table. Now we'll go,
And rest us in your orchard for a while.
The evening breezes will be pleasant there.
For a short time, farewell.

FREDERIGO.

Farewell, dear madam:
I hope you'll find there some — ah! 'ware the step.

GIANA.

'Tis but an awkward entrance, sir, indeed.

FREDERIGO.

You'll find some books in the arbor, where you rest.
They are books of poetry. If I remember,
You loved such stories once, thinking they brought
Man to a true and fine humanity.

GIANA.

You've a good memory, signior. That must be —
Stay, let me count: ay, some six years ago.

FREDERIGO.

About the time.

GIANA.

You were thought heir, I think,
Then, to the Count Filippo: you displeased him:
How was 't?

FREDERIGO.

Oh! some mere trifle. I forget.

GIANA.

Nay, tell me; for some said you were ungrateful.

FREDERIGO.

I could not marry to his wish.

GIANA.

Was it so?

FREDERIGO.

Thus simply: nothing more, believe it.

GIANA.

I did not know it. Not marry to his wish!
[*Exit.*

FREDERIGO.

She comes to dine; to dine with me, who am
A beggar. Now, what shall I do to give
This idol entertainment? Not a coin!

Not one, by Heav'n, and not a friend to lend
The veriest trifle to a wretch like me.
And she has descended from her pride too — no;
No, no; she had no pride. Now if I give
Excusings, she will think I'm poor indeed,
And say misfortune starved the spirit hence
Of an Italian gentleman. No more:
She must be feasted. Ha! no, no, no, no,
Not that way. Any way but that. Bianca!

Enter BIANCA.

This lady comes to feast.

BIANCA.

On what, sir? There
Is scarce a morsel: fruit perhaps ——

FREDERIGO.

Then I
Must take my gun and stop a meal i' the air.

BIANCA.

Impossible. Old Mars, you know,
Frights every bird away.

FREDERIGO.

Ah! villain, he
Shall die for't; bring him hither.

BIANCA.

Sir? What can you mean?
Our falcon?

FREDERIGO.

Ay, that murderous kite. How oft
Hath he slain innocent birds: now he shall die.
'Tis fit he should, if 'twere but in requital;
And he for once shall do me service. Quick!
I'll wring his cruel head, and feast my queen
Worthily.

BIANCA.

He is here, sir.

FREDERIGO.

Where? vile bird!
There — I'll not look at him.

BIANCA.

Alas! he's dead:
Look, look! ah! how he shivers.

FREDERIGO.

Fool! Begone!
Fool! am not I a fool — a selfish slave?
I am, I am. One look. Ah! there he lies.
By Heav'n he looks reproachingly; and yet
I loved thee, poor bird, when I slew thee. Hence!

[BIANCA *exit.*

Mars! my brave bird, and have I killed thee, then,
Who was the truest servant — loved me so,
When all the world had left me? Never more
Shall thou and I in mimic battle play,
Nor thou pretend to die, (to die, alas!)
And with thy quaint and grave-eyed tricks delight
Thy master in his solitude. No more,
No more, old Mars! (thou wast the god of birds,)
Shalt thou rise fiercely on thy plumed wing,
And hunt the air for plunder: thou couldst ride
(None better) on the fierce wild mountain winds
When birds of lesser courage drooped. I've seen
Thee scare the plundering eagle on his way,
(For all the wild tribes of these circling woods
Knew thee and shunned thy course,) and thro' the air
Float like a hovering tempest, feared by all.
Have I not known thee bring the wild swan down,
For me, thy cruel master; ay, and stop
All wanderers of the middle air, for me,
Who killed thee — *murdered* thee, poor bird; for thou
Wast worthy of humanity, and I
Feel with these shaking hands, as I had done
A crime against my race.

SCENE II. — *A Room.*

FREDERIGO. GIANA.

GIANA.

You think it strange that I should visit you?

FREDERIGO.

No, madam, no.

GIANA.

You must; ev'n I myself
Must own the visit strange. It is most strange.

FREDERIGO.

I am most grateful for it.

GIANA.

Hear me, first.
What think you brought me hither? I've a suit
That presses, and I look to you to grant it.

FREDERIGO.

'Tis but to name it, for you may command

My life, my service. Oh! but you know this:
You injure when you doubt.

GIANA.

I do not doubt.
Now for my errand. Gentle signior, listen:
I have a child; no mother ever loved
A son so much: but that you know him, I
Would say how delicate he was, how good.
But oh! I need not tell his sweet ways to you:
You know them, signior, and your heart would grieve,
(I feel't,) if you should see the poor child die;
And now he's pale and ill. If you could hear
How he asks after you, and says he loves you
Next to his mother.

FREDERIGO.

Madam, stay your tears.
Can I do aught to soothe your pretty boy?
I love him as my own.

GIANA.

Sir!

FREDERIGO.

I forget.
And yet I love him, lady: am I too bold?

GIANA.

Oh, no. I thank you for your love.

FREDERIGO.

Giana !

GIANA.

To my poor child : he pines and wastes away.
One thing alone in all the world he sighs for ;
And that — I cannot name it.

FREDERIGO.

Is it mine ?

GIANA.

It is, it is : I shame to ask 't.

FREDERIGO.

'Tis yours ;
Were it my life. What have I, and not yours ?

GIANA.

It is — the falcon.
Ah, pardon me. I see how you love the bird.

FREDERIGO.

I loved him, — yes.

GIANA.

I feel my folly, sir.
You shall not part with your poor faithful bird :

I had no right (I least of all) to ask it.
I will not rob you, sir.

FREDERIGO.

Oh! that you could!
Poor Mars! Your child, madam, will grieve to hear
His poor old friend is dead.

GIANA.

Impossible.
I met him as I entered.

FREDERIGO.

He is dead.

GIANA.

Nay, this is not like you. Why not refuse?
I do not need excuses.

FREDERIGO.

Gracious lady,
Believe me not so poor: the bird is dead.
Listen: you came to visit me — to feast:
It was my barest hour of poverty:
I had not one poor coin to purchase food.
Could I for shame confess this to you? — *you?*
I saw the descending beauty whom I loved
Honoring my threshold with her step, and deign
To smile on one whom all the world forgot.
Once I had been her lover, (how sincere

Let me not say :) my name was high and princely :
My nature had not fallen. *Could* I stoop
And say how low and abject was my fortune ?
And send you fasting home ? Your servant there
Would have scorned me. Lady, even then I swore
That I would feast you daintily : — I did.
My noble Mars, thou wast a glorious dish
Which Juno might have tasted.

GIANA.

What is this ?
We feasted on your noble bird ? Good bird !

FREDERIGO.

He has redeemed my credit.

GIANA (*after a pause*).

You have done
A princely thing, Frederigo. If I e'er
Forget it, may I not know happiness.
Signior, you have a noble delicate mind,
A heart such as in hours of pain or peril
Methinks I could repose on.

FREDERIGO.

Oh ! Giana !

GIANA.

I have a child who loves you. For his mother

You've wrought a way into her inmost heart.
Can she requite you?

FREDERIGO.

How! what mean you? — Madam!
Giana, sweet Giana, do not raise
My wretched heart so high; too high: do not —
'Twill break on falling.

GIANA.

But it shall not fall,
If I can prop it, or my hand repay
Your many gifts, your long fidelity.
I come, Frederigo, not as young girls do,
To blush and prettily affect to doubt
The heart I know to be my own. I feel
That you have loved me well. Forgive me, now,
That circumstance (which some day I'll make known)
Kept me aloof. My nature is not hard,
Altho' it seemed thus to you.

FREDERIGO.

What can I say?

GIANA.

Nothing. I read your heart.

FREDERIGO.

It bursts, my love: but 'tis with joy, with joy.

Giana! *my* Giana! are you mine?
Speak, lest I fear I dream. We—we will have
Nothing but halcyon days. Oh! we will live
As happily as the bees that hive their sweets,
As gaily as the summer fly, but wiser:
I'll be thy servant ever. I will be
The sun o' thy life, faithful through every season,
And thou shalt be my flower perennial,
My bud of beauty, my impèrial rose,
My passion-flower, and I will wear thee here,
Here on my heart, and thou shalt never fade.
I'll love thee mightily, my queen, and in
The sultry hours I'll sing thee to thy rest
With music sweeter than the wild wind's song:
And I will swear thine eyes are like the stars,
Thyself beyond the nymphs who, poets feigned,
Dwelt long ago in woods of Arcady.
My gentle deity! I'll crown thee with
The whitest lilies, and then bow me down
Love's own idolater, and worship thee.
And thou *wilt* then be mine, my beautiful?
How fondly will we love through life together;
And wander heart-linked, thro' the busy world
Like birds in eastern story.

GIANA.

Oh! you rave.

FREDERIGO.

I'll be a miser of thee; watch thee ever;

At morn, at noon, at eve, and all the night.
We will have clocks that with their silver chime
Shall measure out the moments : and I'll mark
The time, and keep love's endless calendar.
To-day I'll note a smile : to-morrow how
Your bright eyes spoke — how saucily ; and then
Record a kiss plucked from your currant lip,
And say how long 'twas taking : then, thy voice,
As rich as stringèd harp swept by the winds
In autumn, gentle as the touch that falls
On serenader's moonlit instrument —
Nothing shall pass unheeded. Thou shalt be
My household goddess ; nay smile not, nor shake
Backwards thy clustering curls, incredulous:
I swear it shall be so : it shall, my love.

GIANA.

Why, now thou'rt mad indeed : mad.

FREDERIGO.

Oh ! not so.
There was a tender sculptor once who loved
And worshipped the white marble which he shaped,
Till, as the story goes, the Cyprus' queen,
Or some such fine kind-hearted deity,
Touched the pale stone with life, and it became
Pygmalion's bride : but thee — on whom
Nature had lavished all her wealth before,
Now love has touched with beauty : doubly fit

For human worship thou, thou — let me pause;
My breath is gone.

GIANA.

With talking!

FREDERIGO.

With delight.
But I may worship thee in silence, still.

GIANA.

The night is come; and I must go; farewell!
Until to-morrow.

FREDERIGO.

Oh! not yet, not yet.
Behold! the moon is up, the bright-eyed moon,
And sheds her soft delicious light on us,
True lovers re-united. Why she smiles,
And bids you tarry. Will you disobey
The Lady of the Sky?

GIANA.

Nay, I must go.

FREDERIGO.

Then we will go together.

GIANA.

Not to-night.
My servants wait my coming; not far off.

FREDERIGO.

A few more words, and then I'll part with thee,
For one long night: to-morrow bid me come,
(Thou hast already with thine eyes,) and bring
My load of love and lay it at thy feet.
— Oh! ever while those floating orbs are bright
Shalt thou to me be a sweet guiding light.
Once, the Chaldean from his topmost tower
Did watch the stars, and then assert their power
Throughout the world: so, dear Giana, I
Will vindicate my own idolatry:
And in the beauty and the spell that lies
In the sweet meanings of thy love-lit eyes;
In thy neck's purple veins, which downward glide,
Till in the white depths of thy breast they hide;
In thy clear open forehead; in thy hair
Heaped in rich tresses on thy shoulders fair;
In thy calm dignity; thy modest sense;
In thy most soft and winning eloquence;
In woman's gentleness and love, (now bent
On me, so poor,) shall lie my argument.

NOTE.—The following Song was published in the same year as the foregoing Scene of "The Falcon."

THE LAST SONG.

MUST it be?——Then farewell,
Thou whom my woman's heart cherished so long!
Farewell; and be this song
The last, wherein I say, "I loved thee well."

Many a weary strain
(Never yet heard by thee) hath this poor breath
Uttered, of Love and Death,
And maiden Grief, hidden and chid in vain.

Oh! if in after years
The tale that I am dead shall touch thy heart,
Bid not the pain depart;
But shed, over my grave, a few sad tears.

Think of me,—still so young,
Silent, tho' fond, who cast my life away,
Daring to disobey
The passionate Spirit that round me clung.

Farewell again! and yet
Must it indeed be so? and on this shore
Shall thou and I no more
Together see the sun of the Summer set?

For me, my days are gone:
No more shall I, in vintage times, prepare
Chaplets to bind my hair,
As I was wont. (Ah, 'twas for thee alone.)

But on my bier I'll lay
Me down in frozen beauty, pale and wan,
Martyr of love to man;
And, like a broken flower, gently decay.

Part the Second.

PANDEMONIUM.

PANDEMONIUM.

SCENE — PANDEMONIUM. *A vast Hall, dimly lighted, is seen; in the distance a river of fire. A throne and seats around are vacant. A band of* Spirits *is heard in the air.*

CHORUS OF SPIRITS.

SPIRITS! Angels! Cherubim!
Kings, and Stars, and Seraphim!
Armies, and battalions, — driven
Headlong from the azure Heaven,
By the keen and blasting light,
And the racking thunder-blight,
And the terror of The Ban,
Come! unto our great Divan!

[*Hosts of* Spirits *descend and rise from different quarters.* MOLOCH *descends suddenly and takes his station.* CHORUS *resumes.*

Come! He comes; the crimson king,
On his broad wide-wandering wing;
As a comet, fierce and bright,
Rushes through a moonless night.

[BELIAL *descends swiftly upon his throne.*

He is come, the angel brother,
Fairer, and yet like the other,
As the thought is like the deed;
Swift, but with unerring speed.

[ABADDON *descends.*

And a third, (amongst a choir
Of thunders,) the sublime Destroyer!
Who from blood did take his birth,
And built his fame upon the earth,
Higher than the victor's glory,
Death-propped and made false in story.

[MAMMON *descends slowly.*

SPIRITS.

Who is this, — a flaming error,
Without speed or sign of terror,
Covered by his golden robe?

CHORUS.

He is king of all the globe;
Master of the earthen deeps,
Where the blind bright treasure sleeps;
Crownèd lord of courts and bowers,
Dicers' hearts, and women's hours.

[*A host of* Spirits *is heard rushing forwards.*

Come! — They come. The air is heavy
With the iron-banded levy.
Every wind is loaded well
With the rank and wealth of Hell;

And the fiery river dashes,
Bounding into double light,
As one by one a Spirit flashes
On the cloud-encumbered night.

[*The light increases: large flowers are seen springing up.*

And, lo! the vast blood-grainèd flowers
Unfold wide their broad pavilions;
And the night-expanding Dreams,
And the star-awakened millions
Clothe them in fresh powers,
And rush to the dawning beams.

SPIRITS.

Come, O come! In this blighted air,
The children of ruin and sin are fair:
We shout and we play,
For Death is away,
Making on earth a dark holiday.
O King of the Night!
Where sleeps thy scorn?
Where tarries thy light,
O Prince of Morn? —
Come! O come!

[*The approach of* SATAN *is seen afar off.*

Come! — He comes, he comes, he comes!
Strike the tempest from the drums!

Scatter music upon the air!
Drown the dissonant tongues of care!
Bid the raging trumpets blow!
Let the crimson liquor flow!.
Bid the Bacchanals shriek and cry,
'Till the maddened Echoes fly
Round and round the mighty halls,
'Till the sound to silence falls!

[*He is distinguished nearer*

Come! — He comes, the king of kings!
On his bright angelic wings,
Which have swept through space and night,
Swifter than the arrow's flight,
Thorough Chaos and its dark stream,
As a thought doth pierce a dream.

[SATAN *descends upon his throne, which expands.*

GENERAL CHORUS OF SPIRITS.

Hail, all hail! — Thy brethren bowed,
Welcome thee from flame and cloud;
Spirits of the wind and thunder,
(Who have lain in sullen wonder
Ever since the great Dismay,)
Stand up again in strong array;
Eagle spirits who face the Sun;
Gods, whose glittering deeds are done
On the crumbling edge of ruin,
When the muttering Storm is wooing

(With love-threats upon his lips)
Earthquake, and the coy eclipse.
Hail! Hail! Hail! — We bring
Great welcome to our exile king!

SATAN.

Spirits, for this large welcome thanks as large!
Hail all! — Since last we met I have been wandering,
Through stars and worlds, to the barred doors of Heaven;
And thence have sailed round the huge globés which lie
Lazily rolling in the twilight air,
And done ye service. On one (a belted world)
I alit, and faced great statures like ourselves;
On one a race of madmen; on another
Women to whom the planets came down at night.
All shapes I looked on; souls of every tinge,
From black ambition down to pallid hope.
Some worshipped the white moon, and some the sun,
Some stars, some darkness, and a host — themselves!
Some bowed before Abaddon's glory: some
Called on our Moloch here, and drank hot blood:
Others to princely Mammon knelt, and watched
His golden likeness; while our Belial (shaped
Like Venus or libidinous Bacchus) reigned
Omnipotent as Death. Even myself a few
Did not disdain.
Spirits! I have sown fear
Deep in bold hearts, and discord amidst calm;
Sharp hate I planted in the soil of love,

And jealousy, that bitter weed which springs
Even in the sky. Pride and revenge I gave
To worms, which else had crawled, whereat they reared
Their curling necks on mountain-tops, and threw
Scorn and rebellious thoughts tow'rd Heaven itself.

ALL.

Hail! Hail!

SATAN.

Since then I have flown across the perilous deep,
Haunted by pain; the crash of rocks uptorn
Sang by me, and the loud mad hurricanes
Roared through the ether, and hot lightnings sought me,
And bellowing in my track the Thunder ran.

MOLOCH.

Still thou art here, unhurt?

SATAN.

Still I am here,
Undaunted and untouched. Now speak, Abaddon!
What hast thou wrought on earth these hundred years?

ABADDON.

That sphere, thou know'st, was Moloch's. When he drove
His red battalions from earth's air, I chained
Outrageous Famine in her den, and fed
The blue Plague till it panted into sleep;
Then to the Earthquake gave a populous town,

And rested from my toil: yet, — to pass time,
I plucked a Seville doctor from his chair,
And, clothed in his lusty likeness, taught through Spain
Averroes and Galen. I talked boldly,
Concocted poisons, and foretold eclipse,
And wed inseparably mind to dust:
So I'd a host of sceptics. What didst thou ?
[*To* MAMMON.

MAMMON.

Hearing of a rich Cardinal about to die,
I lay me down beside the Vatican;
And, when I saw his soul escape in smoke
Over Saint Peter's, I uncased my spirit,
And stole into the scarlet churchman's heart.
His corpse was quite oppressed, so many mourned!
Sighs that would ships unanchor, groans which shook
The Palatine and its myrtles, heaved the room:
To stay which storm I rose. You should have seen
The petticoat-mourners! Two sad sons o' the Pope
Cried "Curse!" and dried their grief; the rest all fled.
How well I did with all his stolen wealth,
Becomes not me to mention.

BELIAL.

I have drunk deep
Amongst the Mussulmans; have unveiled looks
In cloisters that made monks forget their beads;
Blown lax sirroccos on firm honesty;
And fired with amorous dreams the virgin's sleep.

SATAN.

What says our gravest brother?

BEELZEBUB.

I sate beside
A thronèd king, and was his counsellor:
And we knit laws together, such as bind
Strong hearts unto our side, and some which chained
The panther people, as the witch-moon binds
In terror or mute dreams the raging sea.
Sometimes these links fell shattered; but we glued
The fragments with hot blood, and all grew firm.
At last that million-headed beast, whose frown
Doth scare even thrones, the riotous rebel Mob
Rose up, and trod my master-king to dust.
I left his fragments on the city gates,
And flew to join ye.

SATAN.

The same burthen still.

MAMMON.

This picture hath two sides; and one is bright.
Wilt thou hear *all*? — Our gold forgets its power:
It glitters still, looks rich, and smiles; and yet,
Like a false friend, it fails.

ABADDON.

Men multiply

Like worms; but though the strong still slay the weak,
Yet 'tis not much. Some rascal qualities,
Pity, Remorse, and Fear, usurp men's souls.

MOLOCH.

Away! away!

BELIAL.

The church, which late we thought
Grew up too lofty with its load of clay
And toppled to its ruin, now revives.

SATAN.

Ah, Moloch! did I not confide to *thee*
That dusty planet?

MOLOCH.

I have done my best:
Nay, have done well, too. For a hundred years
The wretches have been fighting, men and boys,
Slandering, thieving, lying, cutting throats,
And drowned their passions in a crimson rain.
Fierce Ignorance in college and church has sate
Throned, and (from fear) respected. Knaves have thriven:
Fools have sprung up and prospered: Truth has perished.
A few poor gaunt-eyed scholars, lean and pale,
Have starved themselves in caves, or preached to air
'Bout matters beyond *my* capacity.

BELIAL.

'Tis that, good Moloch, which has wrought this ill.

SATAN.

These imps, though small, are cunning. Thy plain virtue
Is no match for their tricks. Our Belial here
Shall waste his leisure there a hundred years.
Wilt thou have comrades?

BELIAL.

One. Our friend here (Mordax)
Will give me his aid perhaps, unless he owns
Some better engagement for the time. Wilt go?

SATAN.

Speak, spirit! Wilt thou follow our great brother?
Mark! if thou dost, though *here* thou'rt free as wind,
Thou must obey.

MORDAX.

I will obey the prince.

SATAN.

'Tis right. — (*To* BELIAL.) He shall have license and large gifts,
And take what shapes he likes and stretch of power.
Hast thou matured thy plan? Dost thou affect
Any particular quarter of the globe?

BELIAL.

No, so it be but warm ; somewhere i' the South.

MORDAX.

If I may speak ——

SATAN.

Speak out!

MORDAX.

As there are some
Who in the race of thought outstrip the rest,
And pluck the fruit alone, would 't not be well
To make one great example? There is a fellow,
Who, as 'tis boasted, scares the swerving stars,
Hoodwinks the moon, and earthquake and eclipse
Commands by strength of prayer; and he can tame
The tempest, and vast seas, though raging mad.
He untwists dreams. Time he outstrips; and looks
Right through the future. Thus men *boast*. In fact
He *can* read our black language.

SATAN.

How! Who is't?

MORDAX.

A Count of Ortiz, Fernan de Marillo.

SATAN.

He is descended from a meddling stock.

One of his fathers I struck dead with blight
At Cordova. *He* fain would read our acts,
And learn the qualities of death and fire.
Hie thee to Spain, then, Mordax! Fly, my brother!
There's much to do on earth if this be true.

BELIAL.

'Tis truth, indeed. I have some good friends there,
Inquisitors, and nobles, and cowled monks,
Who, with the common herd, will give us help.

SATAN.

And now, good brother! we will say farewell.
When thou art gone, we will proceed in council.

BELIAL.

Farewell! I'll bring some histories for your ear,
At our next meeting. Long farewell to all!

[BELIAL *and* MORDAX *ascend, and are gradually lost in the distance.*

CHORUS.

Fare ye well! Farewell!
May ye prosper, wheresoever
Through the scornèd earth ye go,
Amidst death and pain and woe,
Smiting always, healing never.

Fare ye well! Farewell!
All the regions of great Hell

Echo their wide wonder,
That a god should elsewhere roam,
And the strong unwieldy Thunder
Leaves his black and hollow home,
And along the brazen arches
Pealeth, and the winged blast parches
With its breath the iron shore;
And the billows, in red ranks,
Rush upon the scorchèd banks,
Sighing evermore!

[*Darkness covers the assembly at the conclusion of the Chorus.*

THE TEMPTATION.

"Stand up, thou son of Cretan Dædalus,
And let us tread the lower labyrinth."

MIDDLETON.

THE TEMPTATION.

SCENE I. — *A Street in Murcia.*

The Count of Ortiz *and* Mordax *enter, as from a Tavern.*

COUNT [*singing*].

Wine! wine!
The child of the grape is mine.
We'll nurse it again and again,
Until it array the brain
With wit, or until it expire
In hot desire,
And then we'll drink again, &c.

MORDAX.

Count!

COUNT.

I am well, quite well. The air blows fresh.

MORDAX.

If ever you should go to Lapland, (mark!
To Lapland, where lean witches sweep the moon,)
I'll lend you a broom to ride on.

COUNT.

Ha, ha! — well?

MORDAX.

I will, by Sathan! You shall be equipped
With expedition for a northern journey.
But speak, — and ere the morning stars look pale
We'll breathe above the Baltic.

COUNT.

Ha, ha, ha!

MORDAX.

I'll take thee there upon a goat's back flying:
Look! amongst all those lights. Dost see 'em twinkling?

COUNT.

Away! I could not do an impious deed
Before the eternal splendor of the stars!

MORDAX.

Ho, ho, ho, ho! Now 'tis my turn to laugh.
By Momus, you jest well. Didst ever hear
Of Agaberta, that most famous witch?

COUNT.

No.

MORDAX.

Thou shalt see her. She shall give thee philtres,
So thou mayst change to air, or walk in fire.

COUNT.

Peace, peace! no more. The place seems full of frenzy.
Millions of sparks go dancing through the air:
My brain grows sick and dizzy. How is this?
An armèd phantom seems to gaze upon us!

MORDAX.

That is my master.

COUNT.

What, yon piece of cloud?

MORDAX.

Ay, sir, yon lofty gentleman. Folks say
He was a gambler once, and dared a stake
Such as before or since was never won.
He lost, indeed ——

COUNT.

'Tis gone!

MORDAX.

He came to show
How tenderly he watches over us.
Hark! there are footsteps coming. This way, sir.
They must not track us. Hush!

COUNT.

How the wind wails! [*Exeunt*

DON FERRAND *and* INEZ *enter*.

DON FERRAND.

Look! where they go, well mated, (rake and knave,)
The tavern brawler, and his crookèd friend!

INEZ.

Uncle, — beware!

DON FERRAND.

If the fierce devil still
Sends out his brood to blacken this fair world,
That slave is one; he with the dusk brute visage,
And shuffling gait, and glittering scorching eyes.

INEZ.

But Manuel, sir, has nought in common with him.
The Count of Ortiz, be whoe'er his mates,
Owns something still, methinks, which asks respect.

DON FERRAND.

So! so! You love him still? *You*, Melchior's daughter,
With half a kingdom for your dowry. Good!

INEZ.

I love him? — Well, I love him. What must follow?

DON FERRAND.

Nothing; all's said. The worst extremity
Of baseness and enduring grief is touched.

INEZ.

Speak gently, sir; and speak more nobly too,
Of one who (though now fall'n) *was* good and wise:
Valiant he *is*, sir, and a peer of Spain;
And on his brow wears his nobility!
Why do you scorn him, sir? He ever spoke
Kindly of you; and when my father's fame
And tottering greatness asked for some strong help,
He pledged his honor for his truth, and saved him.

DON FERRAND.

That story wants but truth. If time be given ——

INEZ.

If time be given, he'll force the world give back
Its bright opinion, sir, and show him honor.
Oh! then (*if* he return, and stand redeemed
From his wild youth and be — what he *may* be)
Soon shall the poor maid cast her mask of pride,
And look, once more, love upon Manuel!

[*Exeunt.*

SCENE II. — *An underground Cemetery.*

The COUNT *and* MORDAX *are dimly seen descending a broad flight of steps in the distance.*

MORDAX (*entering*).

Adieu, Sir Phosphor! For thy light, take thanks!
We've barred the world out bravely, noble count!

COUNT.

Where are we? What! is *this* the road? 'Tis dark.

MORDAX.

Ay; but as fire is struck from out cold stone,
We'll pluck bright wonders from this world of night.
One of earth's wisest sons, 'tis said, taught men
That they should seek her subtle secrets, not
In their near likeness, but in opposite shapes.

COUNT.

Ho, speak! Who goes? I thought — but no; 'twas nothing.

MORDAX.

'Tis nought. Look up! This is a cemetery.

Take care, else you may stumble on a king.
Holla! Methought I trod on a fool's skull.
This is a learned spot; perhaps a bed
Of full blown doctors: — they are harmless now!

COUNT.

You are a nice observer.

MORDAX.

Oh! I am used
To choose 'tween knave and fool. Dost thou not see,
There, — a pale stream of light, run to and fro,
Threading the darkness? — 'tis a madman's wits.

COUNT.

Where are we? Let us go. The air is close:
And noises as of falling waters, mixed
With strange laments and hummings of fierce insects,
Take my ears captive.

MORDAX.

O fine harmony!
'Faith, they have dexterous fiddlers here. Who blows
The trumpet honeysuckle in my ear?
Speak out, Sir Gnome. Hush! hark! That gentleman
Who beats the drum must be a cricket?

COUNT.

'Tis one.

MORDAX.

Right, or a death-watch. Now, sir, what's the matter?

COUNT.

I felt a clammy touch, as cold as death,
Flap on my cheek, and something breathed on me
An earthy odor — faugh! as though the tongue
O'er which 't had passed had fed on worms and dust.
Again, — who goes? Dost thou not hear a trampling?

MORDAX.

Be calm: 'tis but some people from the Moon,
Or the star Venus, or from Mercury,
Madmen, or rakes; or monks, — fellows who feed
On air, and rail against our homely dishes.
A plague upon the spiritual rogues,
They always abuse their betters!

COUNT.

Hush, — sweet music!
The air is vital: every pore seems stung
Until it whispers with a thousand tongues!

VOICES *are heard; faintly at first, but becoming gradually more distinct.*

SPIRITS (*below*).

Come away! come away!

SPIRITS (*above*).

Whither? whither?

SPIRITS (*below*).

Come away! come away!
And leave the light of the fading day!
Thorough the vapor, across the stream
Come, — as swift as a lover's dream!

Come hither! come hither! come hither!
Over the wood and over the heather!
Where winds are dying
Along the deep;
Where rivers are lying
Asleep, asleep!

SPIRITS (*above*).

We come! we are coming! but whither?

SPIRITS (*below*).

Come hither! come hither! come hither!

CHORUS.

Hark! hark! hark! hark!
A power is peopling all the dark
With wonder; life, and death, and terror;
And dreams which fill the brain with error.
The elves are coming in glittering streams,
Loaded with light from the moon beams;
And the gnomes are behind in a dusky legion,
Hurrying all to their earthen fare:

A VOICE.

Stand, and gaze! for now ye are
In the midst of a magic region!

MORDAX.

Dost hear, Count? Look about? What see you, sir?

COUNT.

I see a vault, — spectral, — immeasurable,
Save that at times its gaunt and stony ribs
Bulge through the darkness and betray its bounds:
And now come countless crowds, (millions on millions,)
Whirling like glittering fire-flies round about us.
By hell, the things seem human! Let me pass.

MORDAX.

Stay, stay, sir; use more patience; you'll dislodge
These piles of coffins. Kings and counts lie here, sir,
Shouldering each other from their places still.
The villanous lifeless lump of clay——

COUNT.

What's that?
Methought I heard the arches crack: — Look, look!
The pillars are alive! Each one turns round,
And scowls, as though the weight crushed in his brain!
Dead faces leer upon me; figures chatter;
And from the darkest depths watch horrid eyes!
Let me come near thee.

MORDAX.

Rest here.

COUNT.

Ha! I feel
As though I leant against an iron shape.
Thy sinews (and thy heart?) are firmly knit.

MORDAX.

Never did nerve or muscle yet give way,
From fear, or pity, or remorse, or love!
Never did yet the bounding blood go back
Into its springs, or leave my dusk cheek pale.
But, I'll not boast at present. Some dull day
I'll tell you all I've done, — since Cain went mad.
Meantime, let's see what comes. How fare you now?

COUNT.

I feel more firm since I did lean on thee.
But, hark! the ground labors with some strange birth.
What volumes of dark smoke it sends abroad!
Blow off the cloud!

[MORDAX *blows, and a Mirror is seen.*

What's here? Methinks I see
A mighty glass, set in an ebon frame.

MORDAX.

Right, sir; true Madagascar; black as hate.
Now, then, we'll show you what our art can do:

Wilt have a ghost from Lapland or Japan?
Speak! for 'twill cost a minute, and some rhyme.

COUNT.

You're pleasant?

MORDAX.

Sir, they'll not obey plain prose.
Whate'er my friends, the utilitarians, preach,
Verse *has* its use, you see. But listen, senor.
— Come!
Without torch, or trump, or drum,
Every fine audacious spirit
Who doth vice or spite inherit!
By *His* name, long-worshipped 'round
All the red realms underground,
I bid and bind ye to my spell!
By the sinner who doth dwell
In the temple like a saint!
By the unbeliever's taint!
By the human beasts who riot
O'er their brothers graved in quiet!

COUNT.

You have a choice collection of quaint phrases.

MORDAX.

I picked 'em up, as men of reputation
Steal musty phrases from forgotten books.

But how's this? 'Wake, dust o' the earth! Are ye deaf?
Mischievous? mad? or spelled? or bound in brass?
Away! a million of you tumbling imps
That jump about here! Hence, and drag before us
A squadron of sea-buried bones. Begone!
Ravage the deep, and let us see your backs
Crack with a ship load from the ooze. Oh, ho!
Dost thou not hear him?

COUNT.

A strange noise I hear.

MORDAX.

It is the Atlantic stirring in his depths.
Dost hear his spouting floods? Hark! Banks and cliffs
Are broken, and the boiling billows run
Over the land and lay the sea-depths bare!
Now shall the lean ghosts laugh and shake their sides,
Cramped by the waves no more!

COUNT.

How the winds blow!

A Throng of Shadows *rush in.*

SHADOWS.

We come: we have burst the chain
Of slumber, and death, and pain.
The ice bolts could not bind us,

Though they shot through our shrunken forms;
And we left the swift light behind us,
The wrack and the howling storms.

A Group of Spirits *descend.*

FIRST SPIRIT.

I have trod the frozen mountains.

SECOND SPIRIT.

I have winged the burning air.

THIRD SPIRIT.

I have left the boiling fountains,
Which, like flowers rich and rare,
Spread their leaves of crystal high,
In the lonely polar sky!

A Crowd of Indian Spirits *are driven in.*

INDIAN SPIRITS.

We are come; we came in legions
From the flat and dusky regions,
Where a wooden God they own.
We have perished bone by bone,
Crushed beneath the giant's car,
While our mothers shouted far,
Over jungle, over plain,
And drowned the discord of our pain!

MORDAX.

You see, sir, you may choose your company.

COUNT.

No more of this; which may be false,—or true.
[Spirits *fade away.*
Let me see one I *know* to be now dead.

MORDAX.

Dost see this tawdry coffin? It is now
A prelate's palace,—Bishop Nunez' see.
The poor at last can come quite near this saint:
Nay, 'round him, now the worms are met in council:
Cossus and Lumbricus are chosen presidents;
The one because he is a judge of learning,
And t'other has taste in flesh. Wilt see your friend?

COUNT.

No, let him rest: poor Nunez! What lies here
Beneath this heap of rough and rotting boards?
A felon's body! Well, what shall be done?

MORDAX.

Kick it, as you would spurn an enemy!
[COUNT *touches it with his foot: the boards crumble away, and a body is seen.*

COUNT.

Ha! Sanchez! Thou false friend! Rise up, ye rocks,

Pillars, and floors of stone! Rise up and crush
The villain downwards! Hell hath let him 'scape.

MORDAX.

This rogue looks paler than his shirt.

COUNT.

Look there!
The name of Sathan is *not* on his brow.

MORDAX (*looking*).

N—o: there's no name.

COUNT.

And yet, in his black heart,
The devil lived, and swayed him like a slave,
And laughed, and lied, and with a glozing tongue
Cheated the world of love.

MORDAX.

What, *this* poor worm?
What, he with his throat cut from ear to ear?
Ha! ha! O mighty man!

COUNT.

He slew *my* sister,
So good, so fair, so young!

MORDAX.

I warrant you

The gallant's sorry enough now. Begone!
[*The figure sinks.*

But how's this? you look pale, sir. Lean on me:
I'll be the reed, at least, if not the rock.
But, hush! strange music, like a swarm of bees,
Seems oozing from the ground!

VOICES *from below.*

Hush! there is a creature forming:
Earth is into beauty warming;
Between dust, and death, and life,
There is now a crimson strife:
Between fire and frozen clay,
Water, ether, darkness, day,
There is now a magic motion,
Like the slumber of the ocean
Heaving in the sullen dawn!
Is the cloud withdrawn?

A VOICE.

'Tis withdrawn!
Friends and foes are met together,
Like a day of April weather,
Beauty hand in hand with death;
What is wanting? — only breath!

The Shadow of the Body of a Girl *rises.*

COUNT.

Speak, ere I look. What comes?

MORDAX.

A sleeping girl.
Yet — round her white throat winds a dark red line:
What can it mean?

COUNT (*looking up*).

Ha! 'tis herself, dead, dead!
Poor girl, poor girl, too early lost! Was Fate
(Who gives to all the wretched store of years)
A niggard but to thee?

MORDAX.

Now, let her pass.

COUNT.

Yet *one* look; for methinks it is (though pale)
A pretty picture. When stern tyrants perish,
False slaves or lustful men, we look and loathe
The ghastly bulks; but Beauty, pale and cold,
(Albeit washed never in Cimolian earth,)
Like the crushed rose which will not lose its sweets,
Commands us after death. She sleeps, she sleeps!
Have you no power to wake her from her sleep?
To give the old sad accents to her tongue?

MORDAX.

'Tis past my power.

COUNT.

I'll give thee ——

MORDAX.

Noble Count,
Dost think I'm bought with gold?

COUNT.

I'll worship thee ——

MORDAX.

Umph! that sounds better. Yet,
I cannot do't; or must not. Wouldst thou have
The dead turn traitors and betray the grave?

COUNT.

Didst thou not swear that I should look through time?
See joy and sorrow? Wherefore drag me here?

MORDAX.

Sir, you shall see the future, if you will.
But, patience! This fair thing must vanish first;
And then we'll try your fortune. Say farewell!

COUNT.

Farewell, my dear one — Ha! be gentle with her.

(*Dirge, during which the Body sinks.*)

Lay her low in virgin earth,
Till she claim a brighter birth!
Let the gentlest spirits weave
Songs for those who love to grieve;

Maidens, mothers, lovers (they
Who have locks too early gray),
Fathers who are tempest tossed,
Widows who have won — and lost!
Children, fairer than the morning,
They who die and leave a warning,
With the unhealing wound, whose smart
Never quits the childless heart!

COUNT.

Now let us look on that which is to be.

MORDAX.

My glass is there. Yet, ere you gaze, think well.
The future ——

COUNT.

Bid it come, as terrible
As tempest or the plague, I'll look upon't,
And dare it to an answer. Methinks I feel
Swollen with courage or some grand despair,
That lifts me above fortune. Quick! unveil
Your dusky mirror, you, lords of the mansion!

MORDAX.

Base goblins, quick! Unveil your lying glass,
And let my lord look in. Now, noble Count,
What see you?

[Shadows *appear on the mirror*.

COUNT.

Ha!

MORDAX.

Two figures, like ourselves!
We're linked together, Count?

COUNT.

True; but *thy* shadow
Wears a strange cunning look and quivering eye.
And the face changes — Ha! from young to old,
From fair to dark — from calm to smiles — to mirth!
From mirth, look! into — Ha! Diabolus?
[*Turns round quickly.*

MORDAX.

What is't?

COUNT.

'Tis gone!
Methought thou didst assume a fearful visage.
Let me look on thee, nearer; no, thou'rt fair,
As fair as truth.

MORDAX.

No fairer?

COUNT.

Wouldst thou be
Whiter than truth?

MORDAX.

Why, — no. In fact, *my* notion
Is that she wears a much too cold complexion.
Now, sir, I like the olive, — or the black.
Then, she was naked, too, or poets lie :
Give *me* some covering, though 't be but a mask.

COUNT.

That was a fearful face I saw!

MORDAX.

Forget it.
Let us consult the mirror once again.
[*Other* Shadows *appear*.

COUNT.

Heaven! 'tis herself, my love, my dear, dear Inez!
She *will* be mine. After Love's fears and pains,
The god sits crowned with roses! What are *they* ?

MORDAX.

Your children.

COUNT.

Both ? — How fair! no lily fairer.
See, with what matron smiles the mother bends,
Kissing their veinèd temples with her lips!
Mine ? mine ? *all* mine ? O, Fate, why did I swear
Hate everlasting to thee ? I abjure
My rashness at thy feet.

MORDAX.

Had you not better
Dip once again in the dark lottery?
Perhaps this spring may change. But see, what comes?
[*The* Shadows *alter*.

COUNT.

A thin shape comes. 'Tis like myself; *so* like,
That, but 'tis younger and more spare and pale,
I'd say — 'twas I.

MORDAX.

This phantom never lived.

COUNT.

I'll call it. Thou ——

MORDAX.

Be still! You must not talk
To that which ne'er was flesh. Unto my ears
Confide your transports. We may talk together;
Though not to them. These pigmies are as proud
As a rich tradesman, or a new-made lord.

COUNT.

Who is the vision? Speak!

MORDAX.

It is — your son.

COUNT.

Forbid it, Heaven! Sickness or want hath struck
This pale thin boy with death. Must he then bear
Youth without blossom? without age, decay?
After all childhood's ills and pains endured,
(Before life's sweets are blown,) 'tis hard to die.
Let him not perish!

MORDAX.

Do you pray *to me*?

COUNT.

I had forgot: methought the thing was real.
But, see, he comes *alone!* Shew me the rest,
All the fair shapes, and she, the first and fairest,
Whose beauty crowns my dreams, whose heart is mine,
My *own!* Not all your juggling tricks can shake
My trust in her unmatched fidelity.

MORDAX.

I said not she was false: she is most true.

COUNT.

O, my fast friend!

MORDAX.

But beauty still is frail;
And what dishonor could not, DEATH has struck!

COUNT.

Ah!

MORDAX.

Stand up, Count! What, fall at the first word?
Why, this is but the future. (*Aside.*) The weak fool!

COUNT.

O thou false friend! (He turns his back on me.)
Is there no hope, no way, no ——

MORDAX.

None; yes, — *one!*

COUNT.

Quick, quick!

MORDAX.

You need but change your livery, Count.
You've served one thankless king in camps and councils,
Have got hard knocks, no rank, and little pay;
Have been *dishonored!* What else need be said?
Push him aside, and choose a better master.

COUNT (*pauses*).

Umph! — he must be a king.

MORDAX.

He is.

COUNT.

A great one.

MORDAX.

He is a king more vast and terrible
Than any one whose cannon shakes the world.
He hath huge hosts, wide realms, and such a power
As the strong tempest hath when it is wroth.
Fate cannot awe him: Death is sworn his slave.

COUNT.

What devil ——

MORDAX.

Hu—sh! You've guessed well. Hark! his name ——
[*Whispers.*

COUNT.

Avaunt! What art thou? Who art thou?

MORDAX.

Your friend! [*The figure of* MORDAX *changes.*
Your fellow, too, who'll save all those you love:
But, still, you must be prompt. Your vow runs thus ——

COUNT.

I will not hear him. Ears, shut up your sense!

MORDAX.

Choose and be quick, Count; for you're in some peril.

The Inquisitors have scented out your path,
(They are brave bloodhounds,) and will soon be here.

COUNT.

I care not.

MORDAX.

But they've racks, which change men's humors.
Then, for the things thou lovest, *their* graves are open:
Wilt save, or thrust them in?

COUNT.

Be dumb, thou tempter.
Turn your red eyeballs from me. O, 'tis fable
Black, base, unfounded false: what else? what else?
Yet, if it be, — and I *can* save them thus?
[*A noise is heard at a distance.*

MORDAX.

Hark! they are on thee.

COUNT.

Ha! is death so near?
No matter; let it come. I shake with fear!

MORDAX.

I still can save thee, thee and all thou lovest:
Quick, speak the word.

COUNT.

The word! what word? Speak on.
[Voices *are heard without.*

MORDAX.

They're at the door. Say thus: "*I give my soul* ——"

COUNT.

Stay! stop! What shall be done? Now, life or death?
The grave for *her*, — or love? God help me! Ha!
I'm safe: 'twas a wild struggle; but I'm safe.
Fiend! I abjure thee, (*falls down*,) loathe thee.

OFFICER (*without*).

Open the doors,
In the name of the most Holy Inquisition!

MORDAX.

Ha, ha! the holy rogues! — (*whispering.*) You still may choose,
Life, love, and wealth? or the rack and scaffold? Quick!

OFFICER (*without*).

Burst through the doors!
[*The doors are broken open, and* Officers, &c., *of the Inquisition enter.*

Ho! seize upon him. Ha!
My lord of Ortiz? Sir, Count Melchior heard
You were beset by some fierce enemy,

And sent us here to save you. Raise him up!
Now where's your foe? Seize on him!

A VOICE *laughs.*

Ha, ha, ha!

OFFICER.

I hear a horrid voice, but nothing see.
Spread yourselves out, and search the vaults with care.
Haste, and let none escape.

COUNT (*faintly*).

'Tis vain: he's gone!
Wherefore he came, or who he is, or was ——

OFFICER.

We do not ask: Our master bade us say
He'd speak in private with you.

COUNT.

He is wise;
Wise, good, and gentle, as a great man should be.
Bring me before him: I will try to thank him.
I'd go, but cannot.

VOICE *laughs again.*

Ha, ha!

OFFICER.

Lean on me.

Now let us haste : Methinks strange sin and horror
Tenant these lonely vaults. Perhaps they sit
Watching the couches of the wicked dead!
Come, let us go : to the Count's house, my lord?

COUNT.

Ay, strait, strait, strait : (*Aside*) and strait to Inez' bosom;
Which was (and must once more be) my sweet home!
[COUNT, *&c. exeunt.*

MICHAEL ANGELO.

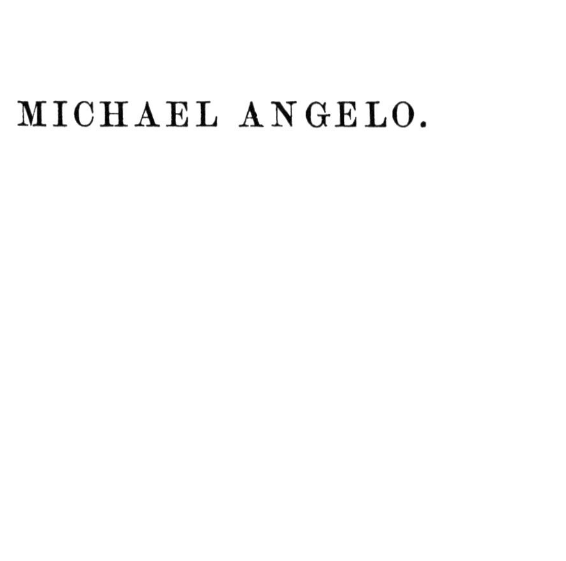

MICHAEL ANGELO.

SCENE — *The Study of Michael Angelo at Rome.*

MICHAEL ANGELO AND PUPILS.

MICHAEL.

So, 'tis well done, Battista ; ably drawn.
Do thus, and thou wilt need no marble fame.

FIRST PUPIL.

Look, Michael!

MICHAEL.

Ah! 'tis bad. These colors sleep
Like death upon thy figures : touch them thus.
This flesh is like a cardinal, red and dull :
Thought should lie pale upon the scholar's cheek ;
Thus, — thus. And now, my young friend, Cosimo,
Give me thy sketch ; nay do not fear me. So!
Why thou hast overwrought this shape, my child,
Cheating (fie on't!) air-travelling Ganymede
Of his boy-beauty. See, 'tis thus : that eye,
Lash't with dark fringe : touch the lip tenderly ;

And hide his forehead all in cloudy gold.
See, let him lie thus ; helpless ; thus, my child ;
And clasp the eagle's talon round his arm.
There, it is done. What think'st thou ?

SECOND PUPIL.

Oh ! 'tis brave,
'Tis brave. Thy eagle is the king of eagles,
As thou art king of painters.

MICHAEL.

Idle child !

SECOND PUPIL.

Shall I win fame ?

MICHAEL.

Fame is a bounteous tree :
Upon its branches hang bubbles and gold.
Which wilt thou have ?

SECOND PUPIL.

Both, Michael.

MICHAEL.

Art so greedy ?
Thou'lt scarcely prosper. Wilt thou be the dog
Who grasped at flesh and shadow, and lost all ?
Bring me that head of Faunus, Giacomo :

That — big as a giant, with the snaky locks,
And the wild eyes, and nostrils stretched and blown.
Ha ! this is right.

THIRD PUPIL.

'Tis like a Titan, Michael.
None but thyself can master these great shapes.

MICHAEL.

Ha, ha ! — There, give it me, good Giacomo.
Why, how thou fix'st thine eye upon its eye :
Wouldst thou wage battle with it, Giacomo ?

THIRD PUPIL.

Shall I not copy it ?

MICHAEL.

Surely ; but take heed :
Mar not the thought which thou dost gaze upon,
Translating it in blind obedience ;
But steal the *spirit*, as old Prometheus won
From Phœbus' fiery wheels the living light.
It is not dainty shadows, nor harlot hues,
(Though flushed with sunset, like Vecelli's gauds,)
Will make a painter. Take great heed the *mind*
Live in the eye, and the wild appetite
Breathe through the bosom and the sinewy shape.
Come near me. Mark ! do not thou miss that turn.

RAFFAELLE *enters.*

RAFFAELLE.

Good morrow, Michael. How thrive thy designs
For the Pope's chapel?

A PUPIL.

Buonarotti!

MICHAEL.

Ha!
Who speaks?

RAFFAELLE.

Thy pupil. Come I in good time?

MICHAEL.

Look and decide. [*Shows a Picture.*

RAFFAELLE.

'Tis grand and beautiful.

MICHAEL.

This visage came upon me while I slept.

RAFFAELLE.

O the rich sleep! Couldst thou not cozen her
To quit her poppies, and aye toil for thee?

MICHAEL.

Methought I lived three thousand years ago,
Somewhere in Egypt, near a pyramid;
And in my dream I heard black Memnon playing:
He stood twelve cubits high, and, with a voice
Like thunder when it breaks on hollow shores,
Called on the sky, which answered. Then he awoke
His marble music, and with grave sweet sounds
Enchanted from her chamber the coy Dawn.
He sang, too — O such songs! Silence, who lay
Torpid upon those wastes of level sand,
Stirred and grew human; from its shuddering reeds
Stole forth the crocodile, and birds of blood
Hung listening in the rich and burning air.

RAFFAELLE.

Didst dream all this?

MICHAEL.

Ay, Raffaelle; and so gazed
On Theban Memnon, that his image sunk
Fixed in my brain. Lo! this is he thou look'st on.

RAFFAELLE.

Sad watcher of the hours, which slowly creep
Through melancholy nights and desert days!
His look oppresses me. — What's *he*? ah, ha!
'Tis Faunus, is it not? That wreath of leaves,

The crook, the panther skin, the laughing eyes,
And the round cheek — or Bacchus? Ah, 'tis he.

MICHAEL.

No; 'tis the wood-god Faunus.

RAFFAELLE.

A brave god.
Stay! — let me gaze upon it. Thus — ay thus:
You drove your pencil round, and thus — and thus.
I never stood before a face so fine.

MICHAEL.

'Tis a free sketch; I know it.

RAFFAELLE.

Thou shouldst paint
Gods, my good Michael, and leave earth to me.

MICHAEL.

The children and the women thou *wilt* have:
What need to ask what thou hast won already.

RAFFAELLE.

Hark! there are footsteps coming.

MICHAEL.

'Tis the Pope.

[Pope Julius II. *enters, with* Attendants.]

POPE.

We come to visit thee, good Buonarotti.

MICHAEL.

Your holiness is welcome.

POPE.

What hast thou done?

MICHAEL.

Since yesterday? — but little, save design:
This head, and that.

POPE.

This takes my fancy much.

RAFFAELLE.

Your holiness is right.

POPE.

So, who art thou?

MICHAEL.

'Tis Raffaelle Sanzio.

POPE.

Ha! and who is he?

MICHAEL.

A painter, holy father; and a good one.

POPE.

What else?

MICHAEL.

Some drawings, which your holiness
Will prize but little. I've been plotting lately.

POPE.

Thine is a tedious art: is't not so, Michael?

MICHAEL.

'Tis hard to compass.

POPE.

Um! — and slow to live.

MICHAEL.

True; — but it lives for aye.

RAFFAELLE.

Right! like Renown,
Which clothes with sun and life the deeds of men;
Building on earth a world which may outlast
Its strong foundation. Give *me* Fame, on earth;
And when I leave sweet earth, a finer sphere,
Where beauty breathes thro' endless summer morns.

Let me have voices, too, heart-wakening words,
All touched like pictures with the soul of thought:
So will I dream over Elysian flowers,
And listen to music, and quaff nectar-dew,
And lie in the light of love, and paint for ever ——

POPE.

Peace! peace! what's this?

MICHAEL.

He *hath* a liberal fancy.

POPE.

He fills his horn fuller than Fortune's.

MICHAEL.

Now I would rather lie on some vast plain,
And hear the wolves upbraiding the cold moon,
Or on a rock when the blown thunder comes
Booming along the wind. *My* dreams are nought,
Unless with gentler figures fierce ones mix;
Giants with Angels, Death with Life, Despair
With Joy: — even the Great One comes in terror
To *me*, apparelled like the fiery storm.

RAFFAELLE.

Thy fancy was begat i' the clouds.

MICHAEL.

My soul

Finds best communion with both ill and good:
Some spirits there are, all earth, which only thrive
In wine or laughter. But my nature seeks
Darkness and Night, Power or the death of Power:
A mountain riven — a palace sacked — a town
Rent by an earthquake (such as once uptore
Catania from its roots, and sent it down
To the centre, split in fragments) — Famine; Plague;
Earth running red with blood, or deluge-drowned:
These are *my* dreams: — and sometimes, when my brain
Is calm, I lie awake and think of God.

POPE.

Michael!

MICHAEL.

A vision comes which has no shape;
None, though I strain my sight, and strive to draw
Some mighty fashion on the trembling dark, —
'Tis gone: — again I draw, again 'tis flown;
And so I toil in vain.

POPE.

But thou must dream
Again for me, good Michael. We must show
A dream that shall outlast the walls of Rome.

MICHAEL.

I'll do my best; but thought is as a root

That strikes which way it will through the dark brain:
I cannot force't.

RAFFAELLE.

What wilt thou paint — *a World?*

MICHAEL.

Ay, its Creation.

RAFFAELLE.

Make it fresh and fair:
Breathe all thy soul upon it, until it glow
Like day. Clasp it all round with Paradise,
Color, and light, green bowers ——

MICHAEL.

I'll make it bare.
Like man when he comes forth, a naked wretch,
So shall his dwelling be, — the barren soil.

POPE.

This must not be. It is not writ i' The Book.

MICHAEL.

Pardon me: I must chase my own poor thought,
Which way soever it turn.

RAFFAELLE.

Still earth should bloom!

MICHAEL.

It should be like the time. I will not paint
Antediluvian Adam when first he sprang
From dust, — strong, active, like the autumnal stag;
But * with limbs *dawning* into sinewy strength.
Nor will I plant the full-blown intellect
On his bright eye, but therein gently unfold
Young Adoration ——

RAFFAELLE.

Right! 'Twill grow and blossom.
Now for thine Eve.

MICHAEL.

Um! Must there be a woman?

RAFFAELLE.

'Must!' — Thou wouldst paint a barren world indeed.
Thou never lovedst.

MICHAEL.

I have: nay, I love still.

RAFFAELLE.

Whom? what?

MICHAEL.

MINE ART.

* See his picture. 'Dominus Deus formavit hominem ex solo terræ.'

RAFFAELLE.

Why, so do I: yet I love women too.
Thy humor feeds one sense and starves the rest.

POPE.

A poor economy. The youth speaks well.

MICHAEL.

Perhaps: yet, the first man was born *alone*,
Companionless, a prodigy like Light.
Birds and the desert brutes awaited him:
Nought else. A world there was (fair if thou wilt);
Yet Eden grew not before Adam rose.
After his birth, indeed, we may have wrought
That pleasant garden, wherein the Devil stole
And tempted Raffaelle's goddess soon to sin.

RAFFAELLE.

Stop there, stop there! The man ——

MICHAEL.

Alas! he fell.
He ate perdition from the woman's hand.
Death for himself — (he was not *born* to die,
But live the lord of this eternal star) —
Death for himself and race, despair and toil,
Peril, and passion which no joy can quench,
Grief here, and Hell hereafter, — these he earned.
Shall I paint all this truly?

RAFFAELLE.

Why not? — yes.

POPE.

Do as thou wilt. Man's life is full of troubles.

MICHAEL.

It is a pillar writ on every side
With fiery figures. Shall we show them all?

POPE.

No: the first fall; no more.

MICHAEL.

Yes, the fierce moral.
That let me do; for I have sketched already
Dark phantasies, and broke up graves, and blown
(In thought) the heart-piercing trumpet, whose loud cry
Shall blast the dreams of millions.

POPE.

What is this?

RAFFAELLE.

The Judgment.

MICHAEL.

Ay, the Judgment.
Look! — In the middle, near the top, shall stand

Jesus, the Saviour: by his side mild crowds
Of followers, and Apostles hovering near.
Here shall be seen the bless'd, and there the damned;
Sinners, whom diabolic strength shall hurl
Down to perdition. Insolent visages,
Born in the reign of Sin, shall flesh their fangs;
Dwarfs, devils, and hideous things, and brute abortions;
Some who make sick the moon, and some who hide
Their monstrous foreheads in a reptile's mask:
Pale Palsy, and crook'd Spasm, and bloated Plague,
And Fear, made manifest, shall fill the wind
With Hell, — for Hell is horror, linked to pain.

RAFFAELLE.

No more. Thou dost bewitch my flesh to ice.

POPE.

No more, good Buonarotti. Now farewell!

MICHAEL.

Farewell!

RAFFAELLE.

Thy figures haunt me, like Disease.
I must go hear some Roman melody,
Accomplished music, and sweet human words,
And bask beneath the smiles which thou dost scorn.
When I am disenchanted ——

MICHAEL.

Come again.

RAFFAELLE.

I will: farewell! Father, thy holy blessing.

POPE.

My blessing on thee, son! Michael, farewell!

[*Exeunt.*

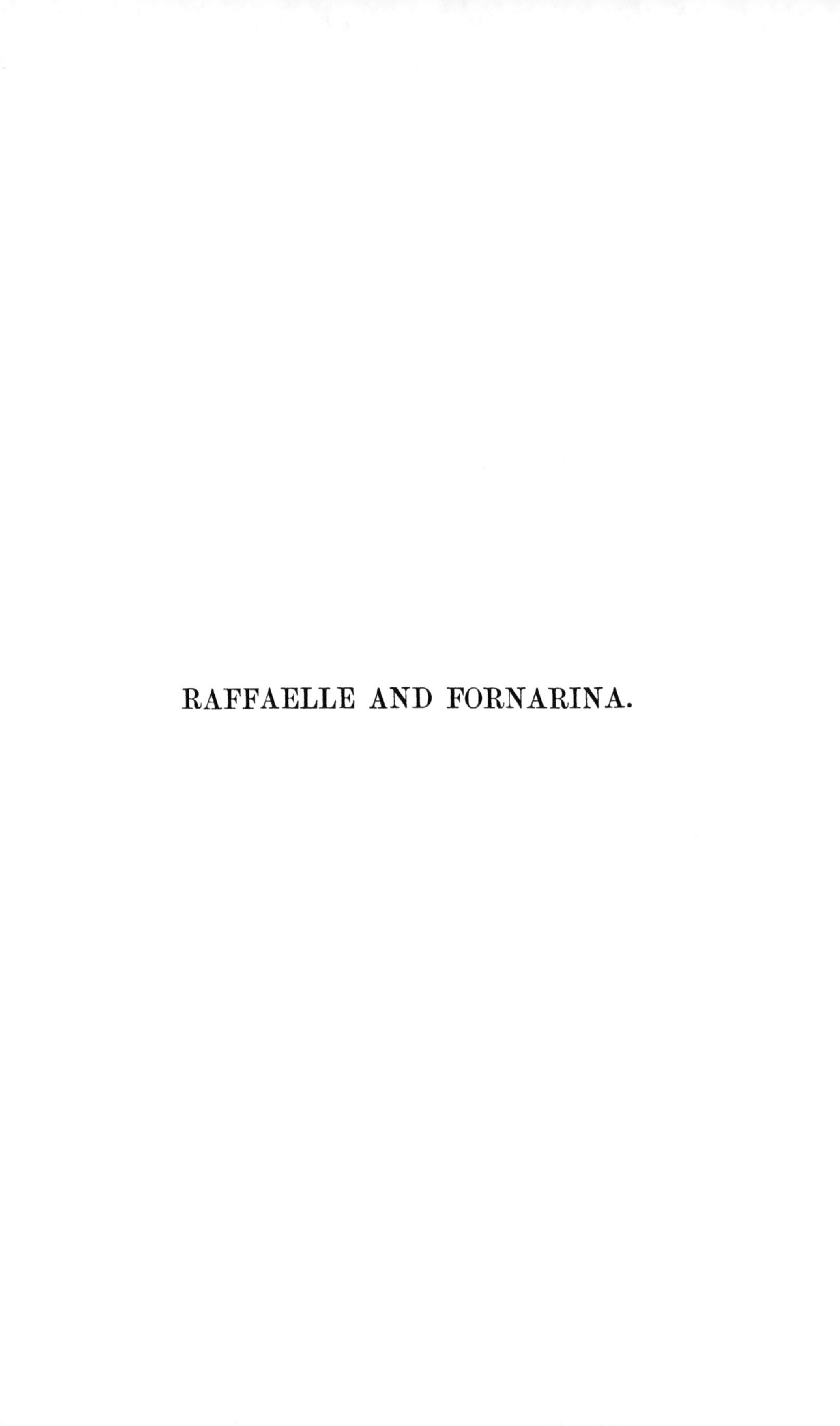

RAFFAELLE AND FORNARINA.

RAFFAELLE AND FORNARINA.

SCENE I. — *A Room in the Palace of the* PRINCE C——.

RAFFAELLE. JULIO ROMANO. (*The picture of 'The Triumph of Galatea' unfinished.*

JULIO.

I do not like that head.

RAFFAELLE.

I am sorry for it.

JULIO.

It is too sleek, too soft, too ——

RAFFAELLE.

'Tis a woman's.
Wouldst have me paint each muscle starting forth?
Or play the anatomist with her delicate limbs,
As Michael doth? Thou'rt wrong, friend Julio.
Here, in this brawny back, thou seest I have writ
Strength and a life of toil: but *this* — 'tis Love's!

JULIO.

I do not like it.

RAFFAELLE.

I have done better things;
But let it pass. I want *her* company,
Without whose smiles my figures turn to stone.
Now, look!

JULIO.

I' faith, that *is* a dove-eyed Triton.
With what a milk-fed glance he winds his shell!
I would have filled it like the North, and puffed
His broad cheeks out like two tempest-blown billows.
This fellow, now, is like a loving shark,
And wears his spirit in his eyes: 'tis good.

RAFFAELLE.

Dost thou not see that, throughout all this story,
The spirit of Love prevails, in many shapes;
In some most gentle, and in others warm,
Whilst in one form, bare lust alone is seen,
The blood's rebellion, the ——

JULIO.

I understand not.
Would all were such as *he!*

RAFFAELLE.

Pshaw! I had better
Have drawn a herd of bulls lowing about
One white Europa, than another such.

Julio, I tire. I loathe this gaudy prison ;
I'll paint no more, unless my love be present.

JULIO.

If thou darest trust thy Venus in my sight ——

RAFFAELLE.

Ha, ha, ha, ha !

JULIO.

Then why not bring her hither ?

RAFFAELLE.

Hither ? I will.
She shall stand here before thee, plain as Truth ;
Less stedfast, but as white as untouched Truth,
Whom slander never blew on. Brace thy heart,
Lest she take all by storm.

JULIO.

What is she like ?

RAFFAELLE.

Her eye is like a magnet.

JULIO.

What, i' the Pole ?
Is it set round with ice ?

RAFFAELLE.

With blushing fire;
With crimson beauty, like the death of day
At midsummer. Her look — O Love! O Love!
She treadeth with such even gracė, that all
The world must wonder, and the envious weep,
Hopeless to match her ever. How I pined
Through months and months (I was a fool and humble)
Till at the last — I won her! Dost thou hear?
She's mine, my queen; and she shall shine a queen.
I'll clasp her round with gems. Her train shall be
Rich as a comet's ——

JULIO.

Art grown mad?

RAFFAELLE.

I tell thee
I'll pave the way she treads on with pure gold.
She shall not *touch* the trampled earth, and do
The base dust honor. I'll have Cretan pinions
Wrought for her, and a barb whose task shall be
To outfly the wind. Scarfs, fine as the air,
And dipped in Iris colors, shall be wove,
In Cashmere and the sunny Persian looms,
To be her commonest 'tire. She shall be decked
Forth, as she is, a goddess!

JULIO.

O rare Love!

What a brave dream thou art! Great pity 'tis
These rainbows which we weave from our dull thoughts
Should perish in broad noon.

RAFFAELLE.

Once, I despaired! (*Painting.*)
Ha, ha! and saw through tears and cloudy dreams:
What wonder that I erred? But now,—'tis day!

JULIO.

Ay, ay; 'tis what we wish it, day or night:
We make our seasons as we make ourselves.

RAFFAELLE.

There; now I toil no more. While I am gone,
Do thou enrich this panel with some tale.
Let it be gaunt, and wild, dim as a dream:
'Twill well oppose mine own.

JULIO.

I'll do it. Farewell!

RAFFAELLE.

I shall be with thee ere the sun's awake.
Be busy, and farewell! [RAFFAELLE *exit.*

JULIO.

I'll do't, I'll do't.
—Now, shall I paint the devil? Ah, ha!—or drag
Misshapen Chaos from his dark abysm,

And stretch him, like a giant, in the sun?
Or shall I tear the blue from South to North?
Or paint a comet plunging through the wind?
This '*Triumph*' of our friend's is wanton soft:
But there's high matter in the sea-nymph's story,
Which might become a painter's pencil well.
He should have drawn the Cyclop, as he sate
Uplifted like a crag, and piped his songs
Of Galatea to the watery shores.
Some say that Orpheus-like he charmed dull stones,
Made ocean murmur, and the airy winds
Took captive; but 'tis *known* he sighed, and sang
The deathful ditties which belong to love;
Calling on Galatea. She the while
Lay mute, and closed (if e'er she heard his strains)
Her soul against his passion. Day by day
He sang, and like the mateless lark called forth
The dawn; and underneath the burning noon
Held mournful celebration; and at eve,
Fatigued by sorrow and wild songs, he wept.
I cannot fill this panel as he bids. [*Sketching*.

The PRINCE C—— *enters.*

PRINCE.

So; where is Raffaelle?

JULIO.

Gone.

PRINCE.

Gone whither? gone?

JULIO.

Ay, marry; Cupid called him, and he went.
You'll find him by the two great lemon-trees,
Which sleep beside the fountain in his garden.
H' 'as brought his brown girl there for summer talking.
[*Paints.*

PRINCE.

'Sdeath! what art thou doing, sirrah?

JULIO.

Um! as my master bade me. I have tried ——

PRINCE.

Tried? ay, and failed. Get thou to Raffaelle, fellow.
Bid him sketch for thee each particular,
The scene, the groups, the — all. I will not have
My palace painted by a meaner hand.
Bid him come here (if it *must* be) with his — mistress,
And paint with Cupid's colors.

[*Exeunt.*

SCENE II.—*The Garden of* FORNARINA, *in the Suburbs of Rome.*

FORNARINA *and* Attendants.

Will he not come?

FIRST ATTENDANT.

Be patient.

FORNARINA.

He'll not come.
The moon, the feigning, fickle, slandered moon
Will surely come; and every trooping star
Be present at his post in the dark sky;
And not a wind that wooes the orange leaves
Will dare be absent. But *he*—false, oh false!
Mark, wenches, if ye love—but do not love:
Yet, if ye do, fetter your lovers fast;
Bind 'em in chains, for love will fail like ice
In summer sunbeams. Trust no smiles, no oaths;
Bury your hearts beneath demurest frowns;
And tremble not, nor sigh, if you'd be safe.
Sing me a song, my child; I am not well.
[Second Attendant *begins to sing.*

FIRST ATTENDANT.

Hark! hark!

FORNARINA.

He's here. Mother of love, he's here.
Come! come away! I'll fly him like a deer.
Now if he finds me — Ah! thou faithless one,
[RAFFAELLE *enters.*
Art come at last? I will not look on thee.

RAFFAELLE.

Then I must punish thee (*kisses her*). Look up!

FORNARINA.

Thou false one!

RAFFAELLE.

Did I not hear the nightingale in the thorn,
Just as I entered? Why, what gloom is here?
No welcome? none? — Ladies! who make our nights
Starry as heaven when no cloud's upon it,
Shine and smile sweetly, as ye love us. Shame!
What is this sullen sorrow, which so dulls
Your brightness? Let rain fall, if rain must be,
And straight grow clear again. Look up, sweet heart!

FORNARINA.

Ha, ha, ha, ha! What seest thou, now I look?

RAFFAELLE.

A world of mischief in those night-black eyes,
And peril on thy mouth.

FORNARINA.

Now, art thou not
A most false lover? Thou didst promise me
Thou wouldst come long before the sun went down;
And lo! he is departing.

RAFFAELLE.

The great sun
Falls from his fiery strength! This purple light,
Traveller of the late sky, will soon — how soon!
Pass to another world. I love this light:
'Tis the old age of day, methinks, or haply
The infancy of night: pleasant it is.
Shall we be dreaming! — Hark! The nightingale,
Queen of all music, to her listening heart
Speaks, and the woods are still. Sorrow and joy,
Pleasure that pines to death, and amorous pain
Fill (till it faints) her song. What sweet noise was't
Came up the garden as I entered it?

FORNARINA.

The sweetest noise on earth, a woman's tongue;
A string which hath no discord.

RAFFAELLE.

Let me hear it.
Come! a soft song! a song!

SECOND ATTENDANT.

What shall it be?

FORNARINA.

Sing anything, good girl. Beauty is beauty,
Whether it vie with swan's-down or the rose.
Sing! — yet not sadly, for the time is mournful;
Nor yet too gaily; that were out of tune:
But sing whatever tempts thee.

SECOND ATTENDANT *sings.*

SONG.

1.

O summer river!
Why dost thou prolong
Through cold nights for ever
Thy sad forest song?

2.

Thou hast warm rich hours,
Wherein thou mayst pine
Underneath the flowers,
Which shall ne'er be thine.

3.

Through them sing and run,
Where green branches quiver;
But when day is done,
Sleep, sweet summer river!

RAFFAELLE.

This music falls on me like silver showers,

And crowns me, now the toilsome day is over,
With sweets akin to slumber.

FORNARINA.

Many thanks!
I think Marcella's voice grows sweeter daily.

RAFFAELLE.

She'll meet pale Philomel in her haunt, and try
Whose tongue is fleetest. Where was't she did learn?

FORNARINA.

Beside a river, when she was a girl,
Mocking its music, as the cuckoo's tongue
Is mimicked oft by wandering urchin boys.
Sometimes she cast her voice upon the winds,
And then strove with the waters; till, at last,
She sings as you have heard. Thanks, girls! now leave us.
[Attendants *exeunt*.

RAFFAELLE.

How soft a prelude are sweet songs to love!
I should be humble, but those sounds have crept
Into my blood and stirred it. After music
What should be heard but kisses? Take thy due.

FORNARINA.

Tush! tush!

RAFFAELLE.

Come nearer to me, — near. Mad Jove
Ne'er loved white Leda with such tenderest heart,
Nor Dis (forsaking his Tartarean halls)
Pale Proserpine, as I do rage for thee.
Come nearer, thou wild witch! nearer, I say.
Be to me as the green is to the leaf,
Crimson to roses, juice to the fresh plant,
My life, my strength, my beauty.

FORNARINA.

I am here.

RAFFAELLE.

I love thee; dost thou hear? I languished for thee.
Ay; I have left sweet praises for thee, — gold,
Thrilling ambition, and crowned delight
Which waits upon bold men who dare and do.
Near, near; I have left — ha, ha! — a Triton winding
His brawny arms around a shapeless nymph,
God Cupid without eyes, fish without tails,
And Galatea naked as the dawn.
What is it that I see in those black eyes
Beyond all others?

FORNARINA.

Love! 'Tis love for thee!
But, what didst paint to-day?

RAFFAELLE.

A team of dolphins,
A brace of Tritons and a crooked shell,
And some thoughts else, — which I forget. These things
Shine well enough for men below the moon:
But *I* have taken flight for Venus' aery,
Where I must rest to-night. Our patron prince
Will wax most wroth when he doth learn my absence.
No matter; he must cool.

FORNARINA.

But thou hast left
Thy friend, thy pupil, him — what is his name?
Thy uncouth, clever scholar?

RAFFAELLE.

Julio Pippi.
Troth, he's as rough as winter. Here he is!
[JULIO ROMANO *enters.*
Why, what has brought thee here?

JULIO.

Oh! princely frowns,
A vulgar word or two, a Roman oath.
Rather than toil for these same well-fed dogs,
With a gold badge and a line which runs to Adam,
I'll visit a wolf, and starve. Your lord, your prince,
Disdains my pencil, sir; commands me stop.
I'll paint him with a flaming robe in Hell,
And give him a dog-fish's head.

RAFFAELLE.

Heed him not, Julio.
If he contemn thy labor, he's a fool;
And so no more of him. Thou shalt paint for me.

JULIO.

I will. Shall't be an earthquake? or a storm?

RAFFAELLE.

Neither; yet something which will suit thee well.
Dost love a marvel?

JULIO.

Do I? By the Gods,
Who dreamt upon Greek clouds Olympus-high,
I love a quaint, wild, wonder-stirring tale.
Let it be Goth or Roman, what care I,
So that each line be stuffed with witchery.

RAFFAELLE.

Then this will suit thee. Now, mark well the story.
— 'Tis said that in some land, I think in Spain,
Rising upon you like an awful dream,
A wondrous image stands. 'Tis broad and gaunt,
Tall as a giant, with a stormy front
And snaky hair, and large eyes all of stone;
And armed (or so it seems) from head to heel,
With a crook'd falchion and enormous casque;

And links of marble mail, which once were brass;
And spurs of marble; and marmoreal limbs,
All bent, like one who staggers. Full at the East
It glares like a defiance, lowering, bold;
And scorn still lurks about its stedfast eye;
And on its brow a devilish courage sits.
This statue, as 'tis told, was once a king,
A fierce idolater, who cursed the moon
And hated heaven, yet owned some hellish sway:
A strange religion this, and yet it was so.
Well; he was born a king, as I have said,
And reigned o'er armèd millions without law:
He sold brave men for beggar gold, and stained
The innocent youth of virtue: he robbed altars;
Ate, like Apicius; drank, like Afric sands,
Rivers of wine; then fell to frenzy. At last
Swarming rebellions (like the Atlantic stirred
To madness by the bellowing of great storms)
Rose up, and lashed to wrath by horrid wrongs,
Hunted the tyrant from his brazen throne;
Hunted him like a wolf from cave to cave,
Through rocks and mountains, and deep perilous glens,
Day after day, night after night, until
His soul burst out in curses. On one dull dawn,
Which showed him, lurking, to relentless foes,
He flung some terrible reproach at Heaven;
Laughed at its God, 'tis said, and cursed the Sun;
Whereat the broad eye of the Day unclosed,
And stared him into stone!

JULIO.

Oh! this is brave.
I'll strain my wit but I will do this for thee.
Farewell!

[JULIO *exit.*

RAFFAELLE.

Farewell! Farewell!

[*Exeunt.*

THE FLORENTINE PARTY.

THE FLORENTINE PARTY.

SCENE — *The upper part of a Meadow near Florence. It runs sloping down to a River, and is sheltered at the top by a small Wood of Olives and Chestnut-trees, and ornamented in various ways. Fiesolé is in the distance.*

PAMPHILUS, PHILOSTRATUS, DIONEUS; NEIPHILA (*as Queen*), PAMPINEA, FIAMETTA, EMILIA, PHILAMENA, ELISSA *and* LAURETTA, *entering as from behind the Wood.*

NEIPHILA.

Come on, come on! A little further on,
And we shall reach a spot where we may pause.
It is a meadow full of the early spring:
Tall grass is there which dallies with the wind,
And never-ending odorous lemon-trees;
Wild flowers in blossom, and sweet citron buds,
And princely cedars; and the linden boughs
Make archèd walks for love to whisper in.
If you be tired, lie down, and you shall hear
A river, which doth kiss irregular banks,
Enchant your senses with a sleepy tune.
If not, and merry blood doth stir your veins,
The place hath still a fair and pleasant aspect:

For in the midst of this green meadow springs
A fountain of white marble, o'er whose sides
Run stories, graven by some cunning hand,
Of pastoral life, and tipsy revelry.
There will we, 'midst delicious cates, and wines
Sparkling and amorous, and sweet instruments,
Sing gentle mischief as the sun goes down.
Quick! but a few steps more, 'round by this copse
Of olives and young chestnuts (to whose arms
The vines seem clinging, like so many brides)
And you will reach't. Ha, stay! — Look! here it is.

FIAMETTA.

Ha, ha! Ha, ha! — Look! how Philostratus
Buries his forehead in the fresh green grass.

PAMPHILUS.

Hail, vernal spot! We bear to thy embrace
Pleasures that ask for calm: Love and Delight;
Harmonious pulses where no evil dwells;
Smiles without treachery; words all soft and true;
Music like morning, fresh and full of youth;
And all else that belongs to gentleness.

PHILOSTRATUS.

Come! Sit by me!

DIONEUS.

Sit!

NEIPHILA.

Sit all!

DIONEUS.

Thus; in a circle.
So, that is well. Now, where is Tindaro?

NEIPHILA.

Ho, Tindaro, our servant!

PHILOSTRATUS.

Laggard knave!
Here, fellow Tindaro! The queen doth call thee.

TINDARO (*entering*).

'Call?' marry! Had she borne ——

PHILOSTRATUS.

How? How, bold knave?
Dost affirm she cannot bear?

TINDARO.

Not I.
Not I, by Bacchus! She can bear, no doubt;
Is fruitful as a vineyard; that's past doubt.
But, signor, *I* have borne on these poor shoulders,
Two trunks — look, look! — crammed full of wines and dainties;
Two lutes; a viol; besides some ten ——

DIONEUS.

Tush! Tush!
Where are the tables?

TINDARO.

On Corvino's back;
And Stephano doth bring the boards for chess;
And Grasso hath the music. [Servants *enter laden.*

DIONEUS.

Place all here.
Thus; in a circle. Now, awake the wines!
And spread these cloths upon the level ground, —
Ho! there: take heed! thou wilt unstring my lute.
Now, where's the viol di gamba? Place it here.
Now, get ye gone unto yon chestnut-tree,
And share your wine in honesty. Away!
[Servants *exeunt.*

NEIPHILA.

Here will we rest, with all our court about us.

PHILOSTRATUS.

Lauretta and Elissa, come this way.

DIONEUS.

Stay, Fiametta.

FIAMETTA.

With Pampinea? — Well.

PAMPHILUS.

Here let *us* rest, tender Emilia,
And on this grassy hillock crowned with flowers,
Rest thy white arm. Now let the violets gaze
Their fill, and drink the blue light from thine eyes;
Now let the thievish winds their sweet wealth steal
From the dark riches of thy hair. Look up!

DIONEUS.

Fair Fiametta, dost thou hear him talk?

FIAMETTA.

He sings, methinks. Or, is't his voice is sweet?

DIONEUS.

'Tis sugared o'er with flattery. Now, for me! [*Aside.*
The nightingales which haunt about these woods
Grow hoarse, methinks.

FIAMETTA.

How so?

DIONEUS.

They lose their music
(Else say their skill) before your honied words.
Tush! what's a rose? I'll crush these gaudy leaves.
How coarse their crimson is beside thine own!
Had I but lilies, I would burn them strait,
As a white peace-offering to thee. Come! wilt love me?

PAMPINEA.

He is a mockbird, and but imitates
The poetry he hears in falser prose.
Turn him to me, and leave him.

FIAMETTA.

No ; not so.
He might afflict thy leisure with his groans.
And shouldst thou chance to love him ——

PAMPINEA.

I ? Ha, ha !
I hate him like a poison plant. Methinks
His very laugh is perilous.

FIAMETTA.

I will medicine 't ;
Not as men steal the poisonous juice from serpents.
I'll let him *talk*, till his last drop of danger
Be spent, and he is harmless. Look upon me !
What ! wilt thou love me ?

DIONEUS.

Ay ; by foam-born Venus !
By all these clinging, creeping, curling vines !
By Love ! I swear it. As the bee doth gather
Wealth from the rose's lip, I'll steal from thine.

NEIPHILA.

You sing too much in pairs. Break up! break up!
And in the place of tender falsehoods tell us ——

LAURETTA *and* ELISSA.

Ha, ha! Ha, ha!

NEIPHILA.

What's that which moves your mirth?

LAURETTA.

Ha, ha! Ha, ha! It is an amorous story
Philostratus has read us, out of book.

NEIPHILA.

We live all here in honest fellowship.
He who is worth a jest or owns a song
Holds it in trust for this community.

DIONEUS.

Ay, no close purses, sir; no hoards of words;
No merry tales: nor serious; no dull songs,
Learned of the cuckoo underneath a pine,
And buzzed in private to a crazed guitar.
All is our own. So, speak, Philostratus!

NEIPHILA.

Speak, without more ado.

PHILOSTRATUS.

I? By my soul,
I never tried to tell a tale till now.
I cannot tell it; nay, if you *will* have
A maudlin story, why prepare your eyes;
We'll have salt tears enow. Once on a time ——

FIAMETTA.

Out on thee. That's a schoolboy's stale beginning.

DIONEUS.

I've heard it fifteen hundred times and more.
Beggars unfold such 'neath our valets' windows
At a penny apiece, and they account it dear.

PHILOSTRATUS.

I knew how it would be. So, come! I'll drink
A bumper of Greek wine and hold my peace.

LAURETTA.

What! vanquished by a man that wears slashed satin?
Tush! thou a soldier! Talk no more of love.

PHILOSTRATUS.

I'll tell it, by these teeth! Once on a time!
(Oh! you are still now); well, once on a time,
There lived a king ——

DIONEUS.

Prodigious.

PHILOSTRATUS.

An old man,
Who wedded (somewhat rashly) a young wife.

DIOENUS.

I cannot hold my wonder.

FIAMETTA.

Peace, you parrot!

PHILOSTRATUS.

Well, sirs; this wife being young, as I have said,
Loved one as young, a black-haired curly man,
Almost a Moor: some women love such men.

DIONEUS.

His name?—I see't. He squinted somewhat, thus;
A pleasant cast; go on, and damn thyself!

PHILOSTRATUS.

She loved this curly fellow: he liked her:
The end was that they met. Each night tall Tormes
Stole to her chamber, when king Philip slept,
And lay upon his pillow. Some time Love
Hoodwinked our ancient king; but he, being prone
Unto suspicion, as most monarchs are,
Soon read in Helen's looks and Tormes' smile
That he was cuckold.

DIONEUS.

'Tis a filthy name.

PAMPHILUS.

'Tis so: but we must fix on bad and good
Names fit for each: we wreak our scorn, methinks,
Too much on words, and pass beside the deed.

PHILOSTRATUS.

Well, sirs: Our king, being bred to tricks of state,
And burying anger in a sure revenge,
Watched, waited, and surprised the twain asleep.
Yet, being in darkness (lest his lamp might scare
That guilty pair away), he could but know
Two sleepers lay there: whether girl or man
Was but a guess. On this, to mark the one
Whose hair was coarser than the queen's, (the man,)
What does he, sirs, but clips — look! shears the locks,
(Then worn in clusters) close into the crown.
This done, goes back and sleeps.

DIONEUS.

An easy fellow!

PHILOSTRATUS.

Well; Tormes 'wakes: and with a yawn — just thus —
Rubs his broad palm athwart his neck. Behold!
He starts: the curls are gone! The queen weeps showers;
Yet suddenly reviving (while her dull swain

Puzzleth in vain, o'er this, then that device)
Bids him haste back, and whispers in his ear.
He laughs, shouts, dons his clothes ; and to the room
Where all his mates (equerries) lie in dreams,
Hurries, and closely clips each sleeping crown
Bare as his own. Ha, ha ! The morning comes,
And our great monarch hath a crop-eared levee !
He looks ; one, two, three, *all* are shorn alike.
Scarce can he hold his wonder : Yet, (being wise,
And wishing not to spread his own disgrace,)
Quoth he — 'Let him who did this act be dumb,
And do't no more ! ' — which said, all go their way.
Then, as the story goes, by slow degrees,
The king forgave his queen : this touched her heart ;
And she requitted him, at last, with love.

DIONEUS.

I do not like your story.

PHILOSTRATUS.

'Tis not *mine ;*
But an old record of a woman's wit.
The moral ——

DIONEUS.

We'll forgive't. Some other time,
A twelvemonth hence, when we have had our suppers,
We'll sleep upon't, while thou unravell'st it.

NEIPHILA.

Now, who drinks Aleatico?

PAMPHILUS, DIONEUS, *and* PHILOSTRATUS.

I—I—I——

NEIPHILA.

Here, ladies, here are grapes, (spread out your arms!)
Purple as evening; figs, and cakes, whose tops
Make dull the whiteness of our frosted Alps.
[*They feast.*

PHILOSTRATUS.

Bring here the foreign wines! [*To the* Servants.

NEIPHILA.

Will none enrich
Our banquet with a song? O shame upon ye!

PHILOSTRATUS.

More wine! Bring foreign wines! Now, which shall't be?
[*Sings.*

Shall't be Claret, flushing,
Dark as rubies, red?
Or Burgundy, all blushing,
Like a bride in bed?

DIONEUS.

Let't be full, and rich, and bright,
Dazzling our eyes with liquid light.

PAMPHILUS.

Then't shall be wild Champagne,
Which soars and falls again,
Crowning the drinker's brain
With dreams all night.

PHILOSTRATUS.

Or Sherry? sparkling Sherry?
Which makes the drinker merry,
With its fine Borachio flavor?

DIONEUS.

Or Canary?

PHILAMENA.

No, that's old;
So is Sack, whose kiss doth savor
Of the wit that's past and told.

DIONEUS.

Let't be full, and rich, and bright,
Like a gem of liquid light.

PAMPHILUS.

Let it be, (if like a stone,)
Like the diamond alone,
Dazzling the night!

[*During this song the tables are removed.*

NEIPHILA.

And now, sweet sister, where is *thy* sad story?
For sad it must be, if thy mind doth speak
Its natural music, and no erring star
Bewitch thee to unhealthy merriment.

PAMPHILUS.

I do not think with you: a merry story,
Methinks, is harmless as a tale that's sad.
Yet, speak, Emilia!

EMILIA.

Once,—in Florence, here,
In that part which looks toward the hills Pistoian,
There dwelt a lady. She was very fair,
Young, rich, a maiden, noble, tender, free.

DIONEUS.

O Jupiter!

PHILOSTRATUS.

O Vulcan, hammer me i' the head!
I'm budding.

DIONEUS.

What! i' the head? he must have horns.
Is he a goat? or——

PHILOSTRATUS.

Peace! my love's a budding,
Crimsoning, all blushes, like a three days' bride.

NEIPHILA.

Silence in court! Say on, Emilia.
Was she loved, this lady?

EMILIA.

By two noble youths:
Guidotto one, a high-born Cremonese,
And one a Pavian, Mutio Imola.
Both dwelt in Florence, where this lady came
With old Certaldo, when those tedious wars
Which vexed the city slept, and men were free
To come from exile to their natural homes.

PHILOSTRATUS.

Call me her name! My head could never bear
These vague surmisings. 'Lady'—was she tall?
Meek? fair? Give me her *name*, and strait I see her:
Else she is but a sound.

EMILIA.

'Twas Agatha.
And very fair she was, and very meek;
Tall too, and bent her as yon poplar bows
To the sweet music of the river airs:
And so it was she whispered.

PHILOSTRATUS.

What, in music!

EMILIA.

Ay, sir; for what is music, if sweet words
Rising from tender fancies be not so?
Methinks there is no sound so gentle, none,
Not even the South-wind young, when first he comes
Wooing the lemon flowers, for whom he leaves
The coasts of Baiæ; not melodious springs,
Though heard i' the stillness of their native hills;
Not the rich viol, trump, cymbal, nor horn,
Guitar nor cittern, nor the pining flute,
Are half so sweet as tender human words.

PAMPHILUS.

Thou'rt right, dear lady. Pity speaks to grief
More sweetly than a band of instruments;
And a friend's welcome, or a smiling kiss,
Outflourishes the cornet's bridal note.

PHILOSTRATUS.

Go on, go on!

EMILIA.

These rival youths were friends;
Till Love, which *should* be free from all harsh thoughts,
Set hate between them. Then, rank jealous cares
Sprang up, and with them many a sharp device,
Plots, quarrels, serenades, wherein the sword
Outmatched the cittern. Each had potent friends:
One band the guardian sued, and one the maid;

But neither prospered. In the meantime, the youths
Tired of complaints, and fights which bred but blows,
Resolved to steal what fortune held from them.
One bought the serving-woman's soul with gold,
While mischief won the man. Thus, each had help.
But, tedious 'twere to speak, from day to day,
Of feasts, and watchings; how the Pavian frowned
Like sullen thunder o'er his rival's hopes;
How with mad violence he traced his steps;
Forced ceaseless quarrel, and out-clamored all
The winds in anger. Even the lady's presence
(That altar before which Love loves to lie,
Defenceless, harmless, all his wrongs put off)
Was sullied by the Pavian's contumely.

PAMPHILUS.

What did Guidotto?

EMILIA.

When his rival left
Certaldo's palace, *he* — whose gold had won
The lady's serving-maid to help his suit —
Stole, ushered by the lamping midnight moon,
Unto her garden, where, with learned strains,
He taught the echoes all to speak his love;
Complained not; smiled not; but with tremulous words,
And looks where sadness strove with humble hopes,
Adored the lady.

PHILOSTRATUS.

Ho! I see it all.
I see't. What woman yet did e'er withstand
These modest mournful gentlemen?

DIONEUS.

Hear! Hear him!
How he doth trumpet all his virtues!

NEIPHILA.

Hush!
Let's know the rest.

EMILIA.

'Twas as yon jester says.
Guidotto won the heart of Agatha.

NEIPHILA.

Ay; but the end?

EMILIA.

One night, the Pavian (warned
O' the guardian's absence) burst the palace doors,
And with a riotous crew, whose chief he was,
Stood 'fore the lady's eyes. Once more he told
His burning story; once more swore to die;
Vowed, menaced, sighed, implored, yet moved her not.
On this, grown desperate, with one arm clasped round
Her fainting figure, he bore her through the halls: ——

PHILOSTRATUS.

Ha, ha! *Now* where's the modest, moonlight lover?
The twanger of guitars, the ——

EMILIA.

Peace! He stood
Like flaming anger in the ravisher's path:
And drawing forth his sword, he bade him hail,
For he was come to save him.

PAMPHILUS.

What did the other?

EMILIA.

Rushed on his nobler rival; swore some oaths;
Frowned and denounced destruction. With sure hand
Guidotto warded, and returned his threats,
And for each blow repaid him with a wound.
At last, the Pavian fell.

PHILOSTRATUS.

The end? the end?

EMILIA.

The end was (would 'twere better) such as happens
In common tales. 'Twas shown by some strange marks,
Which chance, or nature, in her sport, had drawn
Beneath the lady's breast, marring its white,
And by a story which Certaldo told,
(All well confirmed,) that Agatha was, in truth,
Own sister unto Mutio Imola.

PHILOSTRATUS.

And so Guidotto won, and there's an end?

EMILIA.

He wed indeed the gentle Florence lady.
But for the Pavian; *he*, (who loved so well
'Midst all his anger,) when he heard that tale,
Betook him to far lands or savage haunts.
Some said, he bled a martyr to his faith,
In Syrian countries; fighting 'neath the flag
Of Godfrey or the lion-hearted king:
Others that he had fled beyond the woods
Near to Camaldoli; fed on roots; and dwelt
Somewhere upon the unsheltered Apennine.
Certain it is, a hermit like to him
Was known thereafter. In the caves he lived,
Or tops of mountains; but when winds were loudest,
And the broad moon worked spells far out at sea,
He watched all night and day the lonely shores,
And saved from shipwreck many mariners.
At length — he died; and strangers buried him.

DIONEUS.

Had he no friends?

EMILIA.

In some lone cemet'ry,
Distant from towns (some wild wood-girded spot,
Ruined and full of graves, all very old,

Over whose scarce-seen mounds the pine-tree sheds
Her solemn fruit, as giving 'dust to dust')
He sleeps in quiet. Had he no friend? Oh, yes;
Pity which hates all noise; and Sorrow, like
The pale-eyed marble that guards virgin mould;
And widowed Silence, who will weep alone;
And all sad friends of Death, were friends to *him!*

NEIPHILA.

Is there no more?

EMILIA.

No more. My tale is told.

NEIPHILA.

Then let us seek the fresh green river-banks,
And rest awhile under yon plane-tree's shade.
Our fair Emilia there will touch her lute;
And with a song, where love shall sweeten wisdom,
Bid us take comfort. After such sad stories
What can be heard, save music? — Follow me!

[*Exeunt.*

THE VICTIM.

THE VICTIM.

. . . . [High in the parching sun, where Ganges old
Sweeps by the jungles, and broad billows scatters
Upon the burning shores of Hindostan,
Rose a great temple ; in no puny age
Fashioned, but built, like Babel, 'gainst the skies.
Based on a rock, and cut in granite stone,
Its pillars and Titanian capitals
Heaved their enormous bulks, till each o'erlooked
Wide India. To some God, whose name is lost,
This wilderness of stone was dedicate.
Millions of quick-eyed slaves, with dusky brows,
All wreathed in white, came here in the old time,
And on the prostrate marble bent, and swore
Allegiance to *A Name!* Then, amidst storms
Of blood and tears, 'rose Siva, at whose feet
Widows were slain ; maidens, whose hearts were warm
With summer love, old age and infancy,
Shrank in his blazing altars, and left gold
Unto the temple's saints for priestly prayers.
Then prayed the priests ; and then, while darkness lay
On the dull world, the fierce-eyed Saivans did
Mysterious rites, and their nocturnal songs

Went sounding through the long stone-carvèd aisles
Of Elephanta to brute Juggernaut.
And soon this superstition far outspread:
From Oude to the Deccan; over black Bahar;
From the Arab Seas, across to rank Bengal,
It sprang and flourished; and wherever else
Base human folly crouched to baser guile,
It reigned and made its martyrs. . . . There is one
Far famous in its stories, from whose life,
And from whose death, and from whose after fame,
Some learn a lesson. When the droughts are great,
And their squat idols sit unmoved, the priests
Call on the saintly Muttra. To please *him*,
They burn a virgin, and scream loose love songs,
And curse the Rajah, Dhur-Singh, long since dead.
He, while he lived, wise prince, did good towards all;
He lived, untouched by grief, for many years;
And, when he died, left children virtuous,
A happy land, which owned his rule was just,
And slumbered in the Indian's Paradise.] . . . .

SCENE I. — *A Garden, near the Ganges.*

RHAIDA *waiting.*

RHAIDA.

The sun has set, and now should Meignoun come,
My dear, dear shepherd! All day long he leaves
My soul to wander: but at dark he comes,
Lovelier than night, to his poor Hindoo maid.
Look! On the holy altars flames the fire,
Which holy priests now feed with myrrh and flowers:
That is his signal — hark! he comes, he comes!
No, — no: O, faithless shepherd! 'tis the rush
Of the great Ganges, who doth love her lord
(Her ocean husband) more than thou lov'st *me.*
Fond fool, he will not come; yet, soft! — he's here!
He *is* here, and I wrong him. O Meignoun!

MEIGNOUN *enters.*

MEIGNOUN.

My heart! my dear one!

RHAIDA.

My — my *own!* (*falls into his arms.*) You're come?

MEIGNOUN.

Ay, but I soon must leave thee, sweet Hindoo!
With scarce a kiss from thy rich lip, must I
Seek the great City. Even now, my friends
Are waiting for me on the river banks;
And I must sigh — farewell!

RHAIDA.

Go, — go: farewell!

MEIGNOUN.

To-morrow I will come to thee betimes;
And I will bring with me the nuptial lamp,
And the bright bridal jewels ——

RHAIDA.

Come *thyself.*
O thou, who art beyond all gems to *me!*
Bring me thyself; or (if thou wilt aught else),
E'en bring one lotus lily for my breast,
And swear upon't that thou wilt love me ever.

MEIGNOUN.

I'll do't, thou jealous girl; yet I *have* sworn,
A thousand times already, 'neath the stars,
To love, — and I *do* love thee.

RHAIDA.

Swear't again.
Never too often can a lover vow:
So once more vow, and I will list to thee
With ears more greedy than the mother owns,

When on her first-born's stammering words she hangs,
And thanks sweet Heaven for Music. *Wilt* thou love me?

MEIGNOUN.

I love thee now.

RHAIDA.

But ever, *ever* love me?

MEIGNOUN.

I love thee, and *will* love thee. Tush! not so
The summer nightingale shall haunt the rose:
Not Kunya (when 'mongst village maids he dwelt,
In his bright boyhood, and did woo, and win)
E'er loved as I will love. I'll bear thee hence
A bride more envied ——

RHAIDA.

O thou vain, vain shepherd!

MEIGNOUN.

How? — but you chide me well: I had forgot.
I dreamt, as oft I dream, and sometimes hope.
A shepherd? that was true; yet, in past times,
The shepherd's sword hath cut its way to power.
I'll come and re-demand thee.

RHAIDA.

'Twill be vain.
And yet, if thou wouldst cast this cloak aside,
And tell us thy *true* name and parentage ——

MEIGNOUN.

Suppose, sweet, I should be that fierce Decoit,
Whose very name is terror to the land,
The river-robber, Kemaun ? — Dost thou shrink ?
Fear not : your Rajah tracks him where he lurks,
In the dark jungles. He has braved the law ;
And powerful hands are on him.

RHAIDA.

Let him go.
You smile ! ha ! what art thou ? Speak ! Have I given
My whole heart to ——

MEIGNOUN.

A robber ? Dream not so.
Yet, — being a robber, he's a potent one ;
Next to your prince in power. But I must go :
And, ere I go, one word of your fierce father :
I swore (as thou rememberest) to come back,
And from his lips force gentler words. Now, mark !
That hour is near ; and, for the subtle slave
Who whispered lies in thy harsh father's ear,
I'll bring *his* fit reward.

RHAIDA.

He is too base ——

MEIGNOUN.

For anger, not for justice. Then, he mocks
At my revenge ! Methinks he laughs too early.

I wait my time: in hate, sweet, as in love,
Thy shepherd's constant. On black Muttra's head
I promised vengeance: I will keep my word.

[Voices *are heard singing at a distance.*

Hark! my companions call me: I must go.
I had forgot all time in thy sweet presence.
Farewell! The wind is rising.

RHAIDA.

Must you go?

MEIGNOUN.

Dost hear the river surging 'gainst its banks?

RHAIDA.

It murmurs like a tender bride, methinks:
"Leave me not, love," it says, "so soon this night,
When heaven looks kind on earth, and earth is happy."

MEIGNOUN.

The storm is coming. If I more delay
We shall not 'scape the ambush. Love, farewell.

[*Exit quickly.*

RHAIDA.

His step grows faint, — and fainter; all is still.

[*Listening.*

MUTTRA *comes out of a thicket of shrubs.*

MUTTRA.

So, he is gone. Come forward; all is quiet.

The ZEMINDAR *enters.*

ZEMINDAR.

Now, now, where is she? Ah, look where she stands,
The fool, still dreaming of that base Decoit,
That water robber, whom I more abhor
Than poison: but I'll wake her. Girl!
[*Strikes her.*

RHAIDA.

Ah, father.

MUTTRA.

Ho, ho! ho, ho! — (*Aside.*) She will burn famously.
Those snaky locks, with which she snares men's hearts,
That tongue, with which she scorns them—she scorned *me.*

ZEMINDAR.

What, are you dumb?

MUTTRA (*aside*).

Not yet: but soon she shall be.
Her ankles, silver-bound, her round soft arms,
Her bosom with *his* white love leaves upon it,
All shall consume: the priests are ready for her;
The flames are hungry, and my heart's ablaze
With a brave fury. (*To* ZEMINDAR) — Shall *both* die by fire?

ZEMINDAR.

Go in, and wait. (RHAIDA *exit.*) What say you? both by fire?

No; *she* may burn, because her blood will wash
A dark blot from my house: but *he* — come near!
I've dug a hole beneath my peepul trees,
And in't we'll tumble him. To-morrow night,
When his blood beats hot, we'll shut him up.

MUTTRA.

Ho, ho!
What alive? alive?

ZEMINDAR.

Ay, full of life and lust.
We'll cool his dreams, the while we quench his courage.

MUTTRA.

I love thee: good! But he will die — *too soon*?

ZEMINDAR.

No: I have fenced his grave all round with stone,
And pierced the lid with holes. Thro' these same holes,
The music of his screams shall soothe our ears.
Three days and nights I'll live beside his grave,
And listen — while he starves.

MUTTRA.

O brave! O brave!
Come, let us look upon this pretty place.
Come on, come on. Beneath the peepul trees?
Was it not there? This is the shortest path.

[*Exeunt.*

SCENE II. — *Same place. Time, the next evening.*

MUTTRA *and the* ZEMINDAR *are passing along;* KEMAUN *meets them.*

KEMAUN.

Stay, stop! a word with you.

ZEMINDAR.

What dog is here?
A Pariah? Strike him down.

KEMAUN.

'Tis not ill said;
But hard blows must be struck ere that be done.
What say you, — shall we fight?

MUTTRA (*to the* ZEMINDAR).

Peace! do not touch him:
'Tis a strange fellow; very brave and honest,
But strange, as you may see. He brings me news
Of matters afar off, and (with your leave)
I would be private with him. Farewell, now;

[ZEMINDAR *exit.*

I'll follow soon. Now, then, is all prepared?

KEMAUN.

Who is that little withered, winter thing,
Whose knees go knocking by the bamboo stalks?

MUTTRA.

'Tis the Zemindar.

KEMAUN.

So! — I'll take his money
With a free heart. Nature has written dupe,
And cheat, and miser, in his reptile looks:
That's well; we'll strip him of his golden skin,
And tie him to a tree. His girl, you say ——

MUTTRA.

May live; yes, — 'twill be better she escape.
(*Aside.*) She touched my humor, as she moved away:
Methought her walk was like an antelope's;
Her eyes are jewel-like; sweet words she has;
Soft limbs, bright ringlets, and a swan-like gait.
My mind is changed; I would not have her burn,
Till she grows old, and then — the wood may blaze.

KEMAUN.

And, if I rescue her?

MUTTRA.

And *keep* her for me,
I'll show thee where her father hides his gold.

KEMAUN.

Good; thou shalt have a third: *that* and the girl
Thou'lt fairly earn by thy bold treachery.

MUTTRA.

How, treachery?

KEMAUN.

Ay, — oh, that offends thee? Tush,
We on the river care not for such things:
We speak our minds and stab; a plain good way,
And saves a load of trouble. Now I'll leave thee.
My rogues are skulking in the thicket there,
And wait for orders. When this horn is blown, [*Gives it.*
I'll come and make the priests stare.

MUTTRA.

Do not drag
Their curse on *me*.

KEMAUN.

Oh no. I know thou art
Half priest, and three parts saint, and all a knave.
Do I not know thee, Muttra? thou hast done ——

MUTTRA.

Bad deeds, I know't, but I do mortify
My flesh with fast, and score my back with stripes;

Have I not lain on the jagged iron, — ha!
Cankered my tongue? and swung upon a hook?

KEMAUN.

Peace, you blind cheat, how dare you brag to *me*?
What! taunt *me* with your virtues?

MUTTRA.

I have done:
Let us not quarrel, who are now allies.
Retire, and wait the signal. Nay, retire.

KEMAUN (*aside*).

Now let me have both gold and girl, and then ——
[*Exit.*

MUTTRA.

The cut-throat infidel robber! — he is gone.
I breathe more freely. He will do the sin,
And I reap the sweet profit: that is right.
When all is won, I'll lead the Rajah where
The villain hides: none know where 'tis but I.

Messenger *entering*.

MESSENGER.

The priests are waiting for thee, holy Muttra.
The victim which you promised hath not come.
Haste! for the Rajah will be there to-day,
And sacrifice to Siva.

MUTTRA.

Say I come. [Messenger *exit.*
'Twill be a glorious day. The Rajah come?
Well, we must wait until he leave the shrine,
And then do our design. Now, what's the matter?

KEMAUN, *entering.*

KEMAUN.

The wood's surrounded: half the Rajah's troops——

MUTTRA.

Fear not; 'tis nothing. He does sacrifice;
And all his Court attend: 'tis ever thus.
Go, hide your men; there, 'midst the underwood;
And when the Rajah's gone, I'll blow the horn.
[*Exeunt.*

SCENE III. — *A Hindoo Temple.*

Priests are officiating, and votaries kneeling.

CHORUS OF PRIESTS.

Pour the attar, — more and more !
Flowers, and leaves, and spices heap ;
Gums, and oils, and odors pour,
Lest the burning altar sleep !
Look, it sinks — the holy flame !
Why is not the victim brought ?
Once, if called, the Hindoo came
Swifter than the flight of thought !

A HINDOO.

I am here, as soon as sought.

OTHERS.

I am here ; — and I ; — and I :
There are none who shrink or fly.

CHORUS.

Why doth the doomèd victim stay ?
Full of sin is base delay :

Quick, or soon shall sound a curse,
Amidst the thunder of our verse.
Call her with resistless voice!

CHIEF PRIEST.

Come!

The Zemindar, Rhaida, *and* Muttra, *are seen approaching.*

CHORUS.

She comes. Rejoice, rejoice!

AIR.

Soothe her soul with song,
Like a silver shower,
Sweet, and bright, and strong:
'Tis her conquering hour!
Let the music steal,
Like a hidden river,
Through her, till she feel
Crowned and blessed for ever!

The Zemindar *crowns his daughter.*

RHAIDA.

Why am I brought here? — Ha! what means the crown?
I am no victim sentenced to the fire.

CHIEF PRIEST.

Come forward!

RHAIDA.

Hark, he calls on some one. Hush!

ZEMINDAR.

He calls on thee!

RHAIDA.

Ah! no, no: kill me not. [*Falls.*

CHIEF PRIEST.

Whence comes this! Was she not prepared? 'twas wrong.
The Rajah will himself come here to-day,
And pray for aid in some great enterprise;
Till then we shall not stain the altar foot.
Take her aside, meantime, and counsel her.
[RHAIDA *is taken out.*

VOICES *without.*

The Rajah comes! the Rajah!

A PRIEST.

Hear'st thou the shouts? he comes.

CHIEF PRIEST.

I hear them, brother.
The bold, freethinking Dhur-Singh, comes, I know;
But here, in our own temple, he must droop
His lion aspect and obey the law.
Hail, Maharajah!

The RAJAH *enters, attended.*

RAJAH (*to an* Officer).

See they be secure.
Health to the priests of Siva! I am come
To share your holy rites, and offer prayers,
Woods, leaves, and spices, (for I shed no blood,
Save that of foes,) before a God's great shrine.
Bring here the basket. Look, I offer these;
Myrrh, aloes, sacred oils, rich sandal-wood,
And flowers, which you confess even Siva loves:
Take them; and pray that I may free the land
(Else all at peace) from murderous men, who've turned
Our holy Ganges to a place of spoil,
Robbed the poor peasant, slain the sucking babe,
Fired happy homes, and wheresoe'er they've been,
Left death, and violation, and despair!
[*The presents are offered.*

CHIEF PRIEST.

The offerings are accepted. See, they burn.
And now, great Rajah, we will sacrifice
A living creature at the altar foot,
A maid who ne'er was wooed, betrothed, nor won.
Go, fetch the victim. [Priest *goes out.*

RAJAH.

Doth she wish to burn?

CHIEF PRIEST.

Her father brings her. On his house a blot

Hath dwelt for a hundred years; no good stays with him;
His acts ne'er prosper; he is loved by none;
His dreams are bad; his peasants starve; his friends—
He *hath* no friend; and therefore (and because
He loves great Siva) doth he this day bring
His daughter for a maiden sacrifice.

RAJAH.

Methinks *himself* should smart for his own sins.
And she?

CHIEF PRIEST.

She trembles. Human blood will shake,
Sometimes, in dread of the last agony;
But we will pray such fault may be forgiven,
And bid her father fast for one whole day:
She shall not die in vain.

Priest *enters with* RHAIDA, *the* ZEMINDAR, &c.

PRIEST.

The maiden's here.

CHIEF PRIEST.

Come forward. Girl, approach.

RHAIDA.

O spare me, spare me!

RAJAH (*tenderly*).

Come hither, Rhaida!

RHAIDA (*screams*).

Ha! — who spoke to me?

ZEMINDAR.

The Rajah spoke. (*Aside.*) Methinks I know his voice.

RHAIDA.

Where? Where? The Rajah? Ha, Meignoun! '*Tis he!*
I'm safe, I'm safe! [*Sinks on her knees.*

RAJAH.

Did they not say this girl
Was unaffianced?

CHIEF PRIEST.

Ay, unwooed, unsought.

RAJAH.

They told thee false, and they deserve to die.
She *is* affianced; nay, she should have been
This night a bride.

CHIEF PRIEST.

Whose bride, O Rajah?

RAJAH.

MINE.
Come forward, Rhaida. Look! I take her hand,
And in your holy temple own her mine.
Priest, seek some other victim.

(KEMAUN *enters by stealth, and mixes with the crowd. The place is surrounded by troops.*)

CHIEF PRIEST (*pauses*).

Mighty Rajah,
I grieve that 't should be thus; but she is doomed!
The God himself, in his own voice, hath asked
A victim, and I dare not disobey:
I dare not offer one of less degree.

RAJAH.

Then must we strait do justice. Stand apart! [*Kneels*
Terrible Siva! if this maid be thine,
Devoted, and not slain by human hate,
Speak to thy servant, who now kneels before thee.

CHIEF PRIEST.

Arise! The marble hath a thousand tongues,
And might, if so it willed, now answer thee.

RAJAH.

Peace, holy man, do I not know 't? The God,
Whose strong divinity is masked in stone,
Is free as air; his *spirit* still hath power
To will, and make his marble limbs obey,
His marble tongue to speak. Is it not so?

CHIEF PRIEST.

'Tis so.

RAJAH.

Then *speak*, O Siva! If thy wrath

Demand this maiden for thy altar fires,
Speak, and she comes. But, if no word of thine
Be heard in answer, I pronounce her — free!
Behold her! She was lured by falsehood hither;
And they who brought her have affronted *thee*,
By offering a false martyr. She is wooed,
Won, almost wed; and by thy awful law,
Is unfit for the altar. Terrible God,
If thou delightest, as 'tis said, in blood,
Yet sure thou lov'st it most when justly shed.
Know, we have now a victim fit for thee;
One who, though priest and saint, deserves to die.
Spare, then, this innocent maid! — Once more, if thou
Speak'st not, she's free. No answer? Maid, approach!
The God whom now we worship gives no sign.

CHIEF PRIEST.

The sign you call for, yesternight was made;
And I did see it.

RAJAH.

Was the victim *named*?

CHIEF PRIEST.

No name: a victim only.

RAJAH.

He shall have
A saintly victim, who is doomed to die;
Doomed by the law and me.

[*Claps his hands.* MUTTRA *and* KEMAUN *are secured.*

PRIESTS.

This place is sacred, Prince.

RAJAH.

Peace, peace, vain men.
Justice is done in heaven ; why not here ?
Bring forth the prisoners. Men, stained black with crimes,
(All by confession and strong proofs made plain,)
Prepare, for ye must die ! Kemaun, thou hast
One lonely virtue, an undaunted mind :
For this (so much I reverence valiant hearts),
I give thee choice how thou wilt die to-day.
Speak, and begone !

KEMAUN.

The robber's death for me.
A tamer end would blot the fame I've earned :
Death and renown be mine !

RAJAH.

Take him away. [KEMAUN *exit, guarded.*
For thee, thou baser villain, death by fire :
That is thy doom, which none shall mitigate.
(*To* Officer.) Stay thou, and see it done. He is the worst,
More base, more false, more without touch of pity,
Than ever I did think a man could be.
One more there is ; her father.

OFFICER.

Must he die ?

RAJAH.

No; let him live; but in a foreign land.
We will not touch a hair that's kin to *her*.

[*Turns towards* RHAIDA.

And now, thou tenderest heart, and loveliest bride,
That ever made the world more beautiful,
Bright'ning with smiles the aye-recurring Spring,
What shall be done with *thee?* Why, thou must go
Unto a prison; look! to these fond arms;
Whilst I, thy Prince, shall feel more honored,—more,
With thee thus near me, sweet,—than were I crowned
With garlands, red with conquest, or now hailed
By all wide India as her chosen King!

Part the Third.

MISCELLANEOUS POEMS.

THE FIRST DAY OF THE YEAR.

As one who enters on a road
The end whereof no sight can reach;
Where they who bear Sin's heavy load
Are numberless (so sages teach)
As sands upon the wild sea-beach:
Where Showers and Sunshine, Night and Day,
Like Ghosts go glimmering on their way;
Where Friends and Foes, where Right and Wrong,
And all that doth to Life belong,—
The shadowy Past, the grim To-come,
Around our footsteps sink and soar;
Where DEATH goes beating on his drum;
And that great Sea without a shore
Gleams in the distance, while a Voice
Cries out, "Let no one here rejoice!"
So I, now blind with hope and fear,
Enter upon thy paths, O year!
Thy paths, which all who breathe must tread,
Which lead the Living to the Dead,

I enter ; for it is my doom
To tread thy labyrinthine gloom ;
To note who 'round me watch and wait ;
To love a few ; perhaps to hate ;
And do all duties of my fate.

MARCH—APRIL—MAY.

March! — A cloudy stream is flowing,
And a hard steel blast is blowing;
Bitterer now than I remember
Ever to have felt or seen,
In the depths of drear December,
When the white doth hide the green:
Not a trembling weed up-peereth
From its dark home under-ground;
Violet now nor primrose heareth
In her sleep a single sound;
All in wintry torpor bound!
Not a sparrow upon the spray!
Not a lark to greet the day!

Hush! — I hear the silver rain
Beating on the western pane,
Singing songs unto the snow;
Calling earth to wake below:
Ah, sweet April comes, who never comes in vain!

In the Orient — light! A haze
O'er the deep night-blackness strays:

Thro' the cloudy pall it poureth,
O'er the mountain scalp it soareth,
Over, through, afar, around,
(Warming all the heart of May,)
Runs the light without a sound,
From the black into the gray,
From the gray into the dawn,
Silvering all its folds of lawn,
Till it bursts upon the Day.
Gaze! From out the living gold
Knowledge streameth as of old.
Gaze upon the sunny river;
Heaven is bright and bounteous ever.
All is beautiful. — I rise;
God is looking from the skies!

THE PICTURE.

UNDERNEATH yon antique frame,
(Carved, observe, by dextrous hands,)
All apart from meaner things,
The thousand-guinea panel stands.

Once, in the great old Moro palace,
When the sunset evening bloom
Flushed the Adriatic waters,
It lit up the golden room.

Strangers, all who thronged to see it,
Vowed the soldier's coal-black eyes
Burned beneath the lady's beauty,
Glowing there with sweet surprise.

From his earnest gaze she looks;
Yet the passionate words she hears;
As when we fix our eyes on books
We hear a tender talker's tears·

And, note well his tremulous mouth,
Her proud sweet smile, patrician skin;
And her eyes that front your eyes,
Reading every thought within.

What a light is on her forehead,
Shooting forwards from the dark!
How the hues of queenly crimson
All her swelling beauty mark!

And the streaks of rich Sienna
That embrown his visage dun;
And the gold upon her tresses,
Blazing like the western sun.

— Read and ponder, gentle Maiden:
And, within this circle, see
All that was, when Love was master,
All that is, and is to be;

Beauty, conquering and conquered;
Strength, all strength and fame forgot;
Pride subdued; Love, Truth triumphant:—
(Ah, what learner knows them not!)

And, besides these truths, 'tis whispered
That within this picture lies
The painter's story, when sublimed
He rose with Love into the skies.

What names they had — these shapes we look on —
Whether, constrained, they fled of yore,
Far away to Isle enchanted,
Idling on some faëry shore;

Or in dark and toilsome cities,
Or within some sparry cell,
In a sunset wilderness,
Loved their lives out, — none can tell.

But our dreams, which lift the Future
And the Present into light,
Give unto the Past a glory
That leaves the lovers' fortunes bright.

THE PARISH DOCTOR.

I TRAVEL by day, I travel by night,
In the blistering sun, in the drenching rain;
And my only pleasure, in dark or light,
Is to help the poor, in pain.

The Parish Magnificoes pay me — what?
Where it only the money, I would not roam,
But enjoy the little that I have got
By my own fireside, at home.

But hunger, and thirst, and pain, and woe
Entice me on; and they pay me well,
When I beat down the devil Disease, you know:
'Tis for that my old age I sell:

I give up my comfort, my crusty wine,
My slippers, my books, and my easy chair,
And go where the paupers starve and pine,
With help. But for this I swear,

I would spit on the fat false bloated men
Who strut on the vestry floor,
And toss 'em their twenty pounds again,
That they squeeze from the parish poor.

Last night, — O God, what a night of cold,
With the wind and the stinging hail!
What a night for a lamb that had left the fold,
And had wandered, weak and pale!

Yet there she was, — on the midnight thrown
By the rascal that bars the gate,
And the lying relieving officer (known
For relieving — the parish rate !).

These knaves, they are high in their masters' books.
Have a sum upon which they draw
To keep up their credit; though each one looks
To be sure he's within the law.

But gentleness, kindness, love — that lend
To the gifts of the heart a grace,
They reach not the pauper that has no friend,
They suit not the guardian's place.

Their duty is known; — to keep down the rate,
And the poor within proper bounds,
And to pay (that he may not be too elate)
The Doctor with — *Twenty pounds!*

ABOVE AND BELOW.

Look forth, into the azure there!
Gaze your soul out upon the blue!
Now, tell me what you see so fair,
And what that fair reflects on you?

Is Love there? — Joy? — is airy Hope?
Dwell they all there amid the stars?
Or, are they still beyond your scope,
Which some terrestrial error bars?

You see nought: but, you say, some dream
Inspires you to sublimer ends;
And that you rise up to a theme,
Which lifts you as itself ascends.

Well! — even here the lily blooms;
The rose is opening in the sun:
On every leaf are hung perfumes:
From every branch a wreath is won.

Beneath this rough rock, stained by Time,
The sparkling brooklet runs and sings;
And half-way up the brambles climb;
And from its top the acacia springs.

The daisy laughs upon the sward;
The violet sleeps within her nest:
Ah!—Nature ever yields reward
To him who seeks, and loves her best.

Now, for a moment, turn your sight,
To where this tiniest worm expands
His emerald armor in the light,
Like a dragon from the haunted lands.

Look thro' this wizard glass, and own
How muscles swell; how pulses beat;
How Life, that wonder never known,
Dwells in this thing, from head to feet;

Dwells in those parts no eye can reach,
No touch—the tenderest—but must harm,
So infinitely small is each:
And yet, the heart's blood runneth warm,

And appetites pervade this shape,
And Love, and Joy, and Hope, and Fear,
(Such as your upward eyes escape,)
God's agents,—all are dwelling here.

Ah, friend!—not *always* gaze above;
But cast your looks below,—around:
Beside you dwelleth Human Love,
And Heavenly Wonders on the ground.

A GARDEN SCENE.

Sing me a soft love-laden song;
Tie up your hair in a tighter braid;
Here let us lie in the cypress shade;
Here, where the feathery fountain sings,
And into the porphyry basin springs:
Sparkling, flashing, along it goes,
Winding round by the sunny steep,
Whereon the quick green lizards creep;
Hush! — 'tis gone to a deep repose,
There, where the rough rose-bramble blows.

Sing me a song, a sadder song;
All about her renowned in story,
Who died to consùmmate her lover's glory;
Took on her soul a grievous wrong;
Gave herself up, all, life and limb;
Trembled a little, and then grew dim;
Martyred alike in fame and pride;
Kissed the poison, and so she died.

Whisper another grief in song.
Where did Amalfi's daughter die?
Why do Moroni's turrets lie

Shattered by Time and the tempest strong?
Left to bare neglect so long?
Out in the wild Campagna, *She*
Wandered to save her soul from pain;
And there, where the poor and guilty flee,
Began the labor of life again.
Her tasks are over; life is done:
She fled with the light of the setting sun,
Into the azure, far away,
Till she met the dawn of another day.

In the Negroni gardens, towers
Many a grave and princely pine,
Within whose spicy darkness shine
Lilies and creamy orange flowers,
And sculptured creatures, rare and fine, —
Marble Deities, each alone,
Born in heaven and struck to stone:
Thither we'll hie in the dusky eve,
And hark to the measures that make us grieve;
Thou thyself shalt unloose thy tongue,
With the sweets of Archangelo's music hung.

Now let us end! — Yet, listen awhile,
With silent heart and a graver smile;
But back your hyacinth tresses fling,
That ravish the sweets that the summers bring.
Hush! the fountain upsprings again;
You may hear the words of the silver rain!

What do they tell of? Friendship long,
With seeds of the Love-flower sown among?
Of Fate the master? Life the slave?
Of love that awaiteth beyond the grave?
So let it be: — My dear delight,
Now let us whisper the world "Good Night!"

PROVERBIAL PHILOSOPHY.

How often deep wisdom, my Cosimo,
  Lurks in a phrase,
Or a proverb, — you hear it and hoard it
  To the end of your days.

I wish I could pour out *my* proverbs,
  Like wine from a cask,
Such as *Audit vocatus Apollo* —
  (Why it comes, as I ask !)

Let me try. — Do not smile, tho' I borrow
  From a Pagan or Turk :
'Tis the end (*Finis opus coronat*)
  That crowneth the work.

Even though in my course I should stumble,
  Remember the text,
Aliquando dormitat Homerus,
  And do not be vexed.

Were I young I might haply do better,
  Do well ; but alack !
Vestigia nulla retrorsum ;
  There's no going back.

I see now the rocks and the shallows,
  And what to avoid;
Vitanda est improba Siren;
  But the young are decoyed

By idleness; gentle and simple,
  They bend to the rule;
Super et Garamantos et Indos,
  Each playeth the fool;

He who labors when others are sporting
  Is scorned by the rest,
Nigroque simillima cygno,
  Thrust out from the nest;

So I sank, overborne by my fellows;
  Yet wherefore complain?
Quis tulerit Gracchos querentes?
  — I cried, but in vain,

Manus hæc inimica tyrannis!
  When a blow on the head
Brought me down. It was thus my ambition
  Was conquered, and fled.

And now, as you see, in my verses
  Few thoughts are afloat,
Rari nantes in gurgite vasto:
  Yet men of some note,

Keep me sometimes in countenance, kindly,
   With impotent rhymes.
(*Indocti poemata scribent*,
   Is a phrase of old times.)

Well, well! He who spatters the absent*
   Deserves not a friend;
Semel his insanivimus omnes:
   And so there's an end.

I said that I loved the wise proverb,
   Brief, simple, and deep:
For it I'd exchange the great poem
   That sends us to sleep.

I'd part with the talk of my neighbor,
   That wearies the brain,
Like the Rondo that reaches an end, and
   Beginneth again.

What books we might spare, my dear Cosimo,
   Paper and print!
That volume, for instance, with nothing save
   Sentences in 't;

No meaning, no story, no sentiment;
   All is a blank,

* "*Absentem qui rodit amicum.*"

Save the title-page, showing 'twas writ by
  "A person of rank."

We might spare the too deep dissertations
  Which nobody reads,
The Essays (on something or nothing)
  Which nobody needs.

We might spare,—ah, perhaps, our own volumes,—
  The bookseller's grief,
Had we courage to spring from the limbo,
  And dare to be brief.

CELATA VIRTUS.

You give me praise for what I do;
You blame me for what's left undone:
Alas how little is piercèd through, —
How little known of the lost or won,
Under the Sun.

My dear friend here, (would I possessed
His genius — subtle, deep, divine!)
You judge his motion by his rest:
You sound him without length of line,
And miss the mine.

For every common thought I print,
How many a better lurks unsaid,
That wants the stamp, and leaves the mint
Unhonored by the monarch's head,
And good as dead.

How many a towering tree hath sprung
From seeds which wingèd wanderers spill;
How many a daily deed is sung
As good, which hath its source in ill,
Do what we will.

Our world opinions, half alloy,
Pass well: the rest aside are thrown:
And inmost deepest notes of joy
Move not; their own great meaning known
To the heart alone!

Let's live our life then as we may;
Let's think, — as oft we've thought, in sooth,
Careless what passers by may say;
Kind to our kind, in age, in youth,
And true to truth.

AN ACQUAINTANCE.

I do not love you — I do not hate:
A something, 'tween hate and love, is thine.
I have given you — such as it is — a piece,
A *little* piece, of this heart of mine:

A morsel of gold, — but massed and mixed
With silver and iron, and clay beside;
It softens your own heart not a jot:
It pampers — a little, perhaps, — your pride.

You proffer me, now and then, words so kind!
Yet I think, for a purpose, you'd touch — just touch
My throat with your dagger, — then heal the gash;
Not glad — scarce sorry — you'd hurt me much.

You would strike me to death, when the ill blood flies
To your brain, and the riotous pulse begins
To beat; but that I have a *Secret* lies
Down in the dark, amidst all my sins;

And with *This* I have always a master's power,
To keep within bounds your treacherous will;
And with this I shall conquer your evil hour,
And tame your heart, — till your heart be still.

Therefore, and because I must mix with men
Who are scarcely my friends (for a friend is rare),
I shall venture within your circle again,
And be seen with you taking the noon-day air.

Thus far; no farther. I give my *love*
Where only my heart points out the man;
Then I give, as I give to my God above,
Love, intellect, friendship, — all I can.

No stint; no subterfuge. Time and thought,
Heart, fortune, — a river that knows no end,
All (gold from the mine and gold that's wrought)
Belong to the man that I call my friend.

EX FUMO.

I.

FAR down in the depths of our city
  There hideth a lane;
Dark, narrow; a twist like a syphon
  Runs thro' it amain.

Each house (once a palace) is blackened
  By tempest and time,
And the o'erhanging stories seem watching
  For underground crime.

Here reigns the dark Spirit of Silence,
  Thro' evenings and nights,
Save where, from yon attic, there peereth
  The smallest of lights;

Where blooms, on yon parapet, something
  Half flower, half weed,
But tended as gently as love tendeth
  Love in its need,

As mother her child when it pineth :
  There dwelleth — ah ! one
Who worketh and singeth and worketh
  Till down of the sun.

Well, — there (where you see), I beheld her,
  A summer ago,
From this garret here, quite on a level,
  Where they crowd and they stow

The old pictures, and tables, and ledgers ;
  I had sought thro' the house
For some proof 'gainst a rècusant debtor ;
  Had startled the mouse,

Had scared the blind bat from her slumbers,
  The spider had slain,
When, lo ! my glance shot thro' the window,
  Where pattered the rain.

I started : — 'twas now *my* turn, see you,
  To tremble and start ;
One look, and the fiercest of arrows
  Went right thro' my heart.

But no figures ! — they tarnish my story :
  I loved her ; I *love*,
As I worship the mother who bore me,
  The heavens above !

My God! will she ever not scorn me ? —
To ask her for more
Is to ask the sweet light from a planet !
I can but adore !

Yet, — perhaps, — if I gave (and I'd give her)
My life in return,
She would not *quite* scorn, — and she seemeth
Too gentle to spurn.

* * * * * * *

II.

Fate has blessed me. Look ! Would you believe
(I am such as you see)
That fate should have granted the angel
That sits on my knee ?

'Tis our child ; yes, the child of the maiden
Who sewed as she sung ;
My wife — my belovèd. She shut not
Her ear to my tongue ;

But gave up the wealth of her beauty,
The grace of her youth,
To my prayer — to the pain of my passion,
The strength of my truth.

In the front of the attic she dwelt in
  Still blooms the poor flower;
And within it my fancy still blossometh
  Hour by hour!

Ay, often I swerve from the joys
  Of my garden, with gleams
Of the sun, to go back to the blackened
  Old houses; — and Dreams

Of the past, when my life was a struggle,
  Fall thick on my brain,
But tempered, and turned to a pleasure
  That springs from the pain. —

How strange, that the time-smitten City
  Should harbor a place,
Where crazy old age is a beauty,
  And labor a grace!

But it all must be right; and Love thrives
  Most in sorrow, I'm told,
As the lily grows fairer and fresher
  The blacker the mould.

PLATONIC.

WHAT say you? — "I like yon' lady there;
She me; no further we intend,
But nurse this friendship-flower with care,
And live and die — just friend and friend.

I scarce know what her shape may be;
Her color — is it dark or light?
Eyes she must have, for she can see;
Haply you'll tell me they are bright.

It is the MIND which I admire,
The intellectual virtuous soul,
The pale pure splendor without fire,
That lightens up the perfect whole.

In what fair guise the soul is drest,
In rustic beauty, courtly grace,
What heed? I care not for the rest,
So Intellect hath its thronèd place."

— Peace! Ignorant of the good and bright!
Blind scorner of the gifts of God,
Following whose footsteps came the Light,
While Beauty blossomed as he trod.

Learn, Virtue is not more his own
Than Beauty : both he gave combined,
Knowing each could not thrive alone,
So in the body bound the mind :

And from the body, and from its brain
And nerves come issuing (how who knows ?)
Those pangs of thought, of joy, of pain,
That keep and crown it to the close,

When Life (its duty done), the strange
Consolidated fabric leaves,
And soaring — elsewhere for a change,
Again bears evil pains, and grieves,
Again feels joy and hope, rejoices and believes.

THE SEXES.

As the man beholds the woman,
As the woman sees the man,
Curiously they note each other,
As each other only can.

Never can the man divest her
Of that wondrous charm of sex ;
Ever must she, dreaming of him,
The same mystic charm annex.

Strange, inborn, profound attraction !
Not the Poet's range of soul,
Learning, Science, sexless Virtue,
Can the gazer's thought control.

But, thro' every nerve and fancy
Which the inmost heart reveals,
Twined, ingrained, the Sense of difference,
Like the subtle serpent, steals.

QUESTIONS TO A SPIRITUAL FRIEND.

When we met, do you remember,
In the lane?
When our murmuring school was over,
All its toils, its lessons vain,
All its pain?

Since those half-forgotten hours,
You and I
Have trod our distant paths, asunder;
Meeting once, — you to die,
I to sigh.

In your home beyond Orion
Do you feel, —
Do you mark what stirs within us,
Strongest in the common weal?
Gold? or steel?

Love? or hate? — Alas, all passions
Make or mar!
Even my life's at best a struggle,
Gaining, whether in peace or war,
Many a scar.

But You! — you whose journey's over?
In my ear
Whisper, — are you happier? wiser?
Better? than when you dwelt here
Without a fear?

Does the Spirit disembodied
Think? — the Mind,
Dragged no longer down from Heaven,
Soar at will upon the wind,
Unconfined?

Shine they now whose light on earth
Was quenched or hid?
What of those who dwelt in darkness?
What of those who only did
As they were bid?

What of men who had great virtues
And great sins?
Show me just the point and turning
Where no longer Virtue wins,
And Vice begins!

Do you love the hearts that loved you?
See and scan
Our poor world which is so pleasant,
When unto his neighbor man
Does all he can.

Which of all our wants and passions
Cling to clay?
Tell me which you carry with you
To the realms of endless day,
Far away.

Divès, who so long oppressed you,
Do you hate?
Love you still our crumbling customs,
As when you argued, early and late,
For Church and State?

Homer — Dante — world-wise Shakespere —
Sons of Light!
Do they stand in power as princes?
Or lose lustre, and take flight
To endless night?

Light and Dark, and Good and Evil,
Heat and Cold,
Pain and Pleasure, Poor and Wealthy,
Power of Virtue, Power of Gold, —
All unfold!

AN INTERIOR.

UNLOOSE your heart, and let me see
What's hid within that ruby round;
Let every fold be now unbound.
What's here? Belief? — impiety?
Good — bad — indifferent? Let them be.

I see the crude half-finished thought;
The scrambling fancies, one by one,
Come out and stretch them in the sun.
And what's that in the distance, wrought,
Clear, round, prismatic? — It is nought, —

A bubble, swollen to its best,
Its largest shape; yet overmuch.
'Twill shrink, I fancy, at a touch:
Yet, I'll not touch it: — Let it rest,
An egg within a viper's nest.

Hatched into life, I see it swell,
Burst, bare at once its poison fangs.
Alas, sir, on how little hangs
My life; your doing ill or well.
Who'd think that *you* would ring my knell?

I thought you were my friend, the flower
Of jolly, gamesome, rosy friends.
Well, here our ill-paired union ends.
I leave you: Should I have the power,
I'll sting you in your latest hour.

No, — let's jog on, from morn to night;
Less close than we were wont, indeed;
Why should I hate, because I read
The spots kept secret from my sight,
And force some unborn sins to light?

All's mingled here, if keenly scanned;
No element is simple found;
But mixed and massed with other ground, —
Air, — water: — So, I'll keep my stand,
And march with you to the evening land.

SEEING.

THESE are the marble stairs (come on!) which lead
To the famous picture galleries; so, take heed!
On every side are wonders: — You will see
Gems to make rich a nation's treasury.
Our Duke who owns them — [Ah, would he could hear!
Impenetrably deaf! Well, we must steer
By sight.] — Observe now, where my finger points.
That is our Raffaelle's work. See who anoints
Christ's feet: How humbly the poor mourner kneels!
How the bowed head her gentle soul reveals!
[I'll write all on my tablets, as we walk.]
— There, by the barren rocks, again she lies,
Witching the admiration from our eyes:
That is *Correggio's* desert Magdalen.
Above, you recognize the man whom men
Worship, old Michael. Those gaunt heads in chalk;
That sketch where two grim saints or sages stalk,
Are his. Beyond, you see a blazing Thought
Of Titian, in his radiant morning wrought,
Ere kings bent down, and courtiers sought his ear: —
In front (Friuli's mountains in the rear)

Are white nymphs revelling in a summer pool;
Some on the moist green grass, drink in the cool,
Not dreaming that the hunter hides so near.

You grasp my arm — you tremble? — Tush, no fear!
Ah, yes; I understand. — Gods, what a face!
What eyes, where Grief and Love thus interlace!
Around that brow what burning locks entwine!
The mouth — it speaks! Those mute words, (so divine,)
Have told the lady's story many years.
Her name is lost! — The painter? He appears
There, on the carvèd frame, — "Giorgione." None
Now dip their pencil in the setting sun
Like him. Who else could shape a dream so bright,
Or crown it with that sad and thoughtful light?
Ere you pass on, note how the smile just dies
Upon her parted mouth, where Love still lies;
And all the world of sorrow in those eyes!
Good, good! I love to see those tears. They tell
You understand the graceful painter well.
Turn hither, now: And let your eyes be led
To Guido's angel, — his white wings outspread;
His hand suspended, — there, — as tho' he heard
(Gazing afar) some sweet seraphic word.
— How the boy smiles as though he heard the song!
Well, God is good, and human faith is strong.
Perhaps he feels the hymn enter his brain
Through some mysterious paths of joyful pain,

Which to our grosser sense are shut. Who knows
The hundred cells where lurk our neighbor's woes?
Who from what cause each graver pleasure springs
That soothes him when the raven Tempest sings?
To *some* the merry skylark's morning notes
Fall sad from out the skies wherein he floats:
And some delight in melancholy sounds;
And some hate music. In their golden rounds
The poets go, striking the vain sweet lyre!
How few they charm, alas! and none inspire.
Breathing amidst the deaf, who hear them not,
They sing, and toil, and die,—and are forgot!

Boy, thou shalt be a painter.—I give him Hope,
That fickle fairy, who will not elope,
So long as in his warm blood crimsons youth,
So long perhaps as he is true to Truth.
Yet,—as I gaze upon these pictures, drawn
Many in colors brighter than the dawn;
Some touched with humor, such as bees might sip
In summer-time from Ariosto's lip,
I think of all the baffled hopes and pains
That men endure to reach some sordid gains!
Some gains?—am I not ignorantly wrong?
My thought must err. The seed of Poet's song,
Of Artists' inspiration, when they reach
That rare expression, which is kin to speech,
Must spring from a deeper source,—some inward bliss,
Some airy ambitious hope,——

But, how is this?
The crowd descends. What, is the day so low?
Then we'll depart. In truth, 'tis better so.
Than wear his spirit down with too much pleasure.
To-morrow we will come again, and measure
Florence with Rome, — with Venice. That being done,
He shall go home and dream how Fame may still be
won.

HEARING.

CHARMING is it in a poem
　　That Refrain!
Never comes the sweet recurrence
Murmuring on the ear in vain:
Sweetest is the song in leisure,
Linking pleasure unto pleasure,
　　Hiding all the pain.

Curious is the sense of hearing!
　　How it bears
You back into the dreams of distance,
Vanished joys, forgotten cares,
Through the starry ether, bringing
Down the orbèd angels' singing
　　From the upper airs.

What, unheard, were Love's own music?
　　Senseless, cold.
What would be the sweet confession?
It might—ah,—remain untold!
What the cannon's thunderous stories?
What our Australasian glories,
　　With their tales of gold?

Hearing! Sight! All-mystic powers!
    What has e'er
Man, in his divinest hours,
Wrought that shall with these compare?
Gifts are they, from Him who giveth
Life to everything that liveth,
Patient Strength that ne'er repineth,
Hope that soareth, Love that shineth
    Upon every care.

PHRYNE.

SHALL you love him? Oh, yes, love him,
While you live — until you die;
Wherefore ask the idle question?
Why your change deny?

When for me you left a lover,
How I loved you, kissed your brow, —
Lips; believed you; too much trusted:
Well, — he'll trust you now.

In the region of his fancy
He will seat you on a throne,
And fall down, a slave, before you,
Worshipping you alone.

All the good the Gods have given him,
All his wealth beneath the sun,
He will give you, — soul and body,
Give — as I have done!

Will you then desert him? hate him?
Scorn him, as you me disdain?
Yes: — he'll leave the world behind him,
Burthened with his pain:

And you then will sail triumphant,
  To " fresh fields and pastures new,"
Leaving in your wake a murmur
  Of what Hell can do,

When the Serpent stings the woman.
  — Oh, sweet Saints who watch above!
Why should harlot folly reign,
Stinging tender hearts to pain,
Fettering with her slavish chain
  The poor peasant, Love?

MAUVAISE HONTE.

I WATCH the house wherein she dwelleth,
 Love-conquered quite:
I watch and wait, till some one telleth
That she is about to break the night
 With her light;

And then — for I know the road she travelleth —
 I steal away,
And meet her. Face to face unravelleth
All that I long have burned to say,
 Night and day.

She moves; the conscious beauty crowning
 Her queenly eyes;
I, with my face of fire, disowning
The coward heart that within me dies.
 And so Time flies;

And Life, which is so short, will tremble
 And fade in death,
Before the love, which I dissemble,
Will dare to tell, in faltering breath,
 All my heart saith.

Still haunt I every path she treadeth,
The field, the lane;
And read—oh, every book she readeth:
And some who see my tortured brain,
Will soothe the pain,—

Will tell me how she ought to love me,
And that her heart
(Altho' her eyes look cold above me)
Feels, thro' her pride, the arrow dart,
But hides the smart.

And then, I hope!—At times a glory,
From some far clime,
Shoots thro' the darkness of my story,
And then I give my soul to rhyme,
As now;—and trust to time.

LOVE. — (Moderato).

She gave him her all, her heart and her fortune.
What did he do with the beautiful pack?
Gazed at 't a little, and gave it her back;
Negligent quite of a chance so oppòrtune.

Blushing for shame, did she call in her brother,
Or her fierce fighting cousin, to punish the wrong?
Ah, no, sir, she wisely broke into a song,
Felt her heart was all sound, and so gave it another.

"Well; she was wise not to pine for his scorning.
She lives?"—With her husband, just over the way;
She sings him to sleep at the close of the day,
And laughs with her children, sir, all thro' the morning.

Yet has she a heart. She has squandered her beauty,
Long since. It fell off, like the bloom of the rose;
And now on life's road she contentedly goes,
And gives herself up, quite, to conjugal duty.

All love is not burning. 'Tis paler and colder
When hunger, or frost, or life's troubles give pain;
It subsides into calm when our life's on the wane,
And hides its small pangs from the laughing beholder.

LOVE. — (Tempestoso).

Press your palms upon my eyes:
Press your breast against my breast.
Nothing, save enormous pleasures, —
Nothing but the vastest, — best,
Now can give me rest.

From the extremities of earth
I come: — What read I on your brow?
Tell me not of forms or fancies:
Love me; as but you know how.
Your lips upon my lips, — now!

What! am I not he you loved?
Gave your heart to? why deny?
Am I changed? are you a traitress?
I'll not part with a kiss or sigh:
Who can love as I?

In your words there lives a music
That can soothe the soul of care;
In your eyes I see a beauty,
(Beauty airier than the air,)
None but you can wear.

All the tempests of the tropics,
Oceans, deserts, have I passed:
What do you think gave strength to conquer
Deadly ice and burning blast,
But to be loved by *you*, — chained fast
Ever while the world shall last?

TO A FOREIGN ACTRESS.

WHAT shall I do to please you?
To flatter, to woo, to win?
Shall I buy your body with money?
Shall I tempt your soul with sin?

Shall I build up heroic poems,
And force your name on high?
Shall I rush in the Hell of battle,
With your name as a conquering cry?

Shall I shoot the untrodden desert?
Shall I twine with my own your name,
In some glory yet unascended?
In some terrible endless fame?

I see that your eyes are a serpent's:
I know that your heart is stone;
That your love is as false as deadly;
And yet — I am yours alone!

Witch — Serpent — pitiless — worthless —
Look down, where I writhe and sigh!
Speak! What must I do — or suffer? —
You hiss out an answer — "DIE!"

PARTHIAN LOVE.

Thy figure I see in the bending grass;
Thy voice I hear in the song-sweet river:
I scent the rich flower, and sigh at thy power;
Wherever I be, thine image I see,
And flee —
Flee thee for ever, ever, ever.

Thou hast too much grace, in thy perfect face;
Thou hast too many darts in thine armèd quiver:
The pleasure I gain is o'erpowered by pain,
So I leave thee, and grieve thee
For ever, — ever.

What is it that lies in thine orient eyes?
What's hid in thy bosom, thou dangerous giver?
Thou givest in vain or joy or pain,
I shun thy perfume, for it is my doom
To see thee, and flee thee
For ever, — ever!

FAR NIENTE.

Pleasant it is, that doing nothing,
Never moving — thinking — scheming;
Idle only, — dozing, — dreaming
On a sward of quiet green,
By the rippling river seen;
Where the alders in a row,
When the morning breezes blow,
Whisper to the plumy boughs
Of an elm, that overhead
Doth a cooling shadow shed:
In the leaves, perhaps a dove
Breathes her little note of love;
Else all silent. — On the wall
Let the summer sunshine fall,
On the meadow, on the mill,
Idle now, amidst the sedge
Thickening at the water's edge,
And upon the far, soft, azure-curtained hill.
Far be every human ill!
Far be tears, far be sighing!
Nothing gloomy; let the Day
Run upon his cheerful way;
While over me and over all
Silver clouds are flying.

Much, indeed, I love to walk
With a friend, in easy talk,
On the downs, in June or May;
On the downs that stretch away,
Far away, — far away, —
From the white-browed cliffs that keep
Watch above the toiling Deep,
Listening there night and day
What the troubled Waters say;
For they often writhe and moan,
From the mid Atlantic blown,
And will tell you ghastly tales,
Of what befalleth in the gales,
Till you steal unto your rest
With a pain upon your breast.

Yet, how pleasant nothing doing!
What is all the worth of wooing?
Loving? — when you may inspire
Warmth beside the winter fire,
Caring nought what may betide you,
With a book you love beside you,
(Landor's verse or Browning's rhyme,
Or some volume of old time
Loved when Fiction, nurse of youth,
Fed you with the milk of Truth,) —
All the while the rough storm rages,
As you doze above the pages,

Half-ashamed the charmer Sleep
Should take you to her deepest deep,
With such wealth before you.
Yet, till gentle Sleep restore you
To your merry morning fancies,
Pleasant is the dream that dances
Up and down before your eyes,
As the misty daylight dies;
Pleasant are the scraps and lines,
That no conscious sense divines,
Murmurs, — sounds, — that come and go
Just as lapsing waters flow;
Now a whisper, like the South
Breathing from a loving mouth,
Then the silence, — softest, — best,
Till you — fade away to rest!

Pleasant all! And yet there streams
Beyond it, like a light in dreams,
Something even the Idler seeth,
When his idle humor fleeth;
Something that the dull brain fireth,
And the ambitious Soul desireth;
Regions where the poet's vision
Openeth into fields Elysian;
Gardens, with their clustering gold;
Castles, rich with pictures old,
Done by famous painters dead,
Ere the Heroic Spirit fled,

Leaving Earth to later glories,
Fitted, each in turn, for stories
That would crown the Artist's fame,
Were he worthy of his name.

Idler! — Let his idling cease,
If he hope to dwell in peace,
Such a peace as Labor gives
Unto every one that lives;
Let him seek, — nor idly, seek,
But wear his toil upon his cheek:
What he seeketh he shall find,
Food for every mood of mind;
Learning culled from antique bowers;
Science, sweet in midnight hours;
Music, silvering down in showers;
All the poets wise have brought
From the inner realms of Thought;
All that the master, Love, can teach, amidst a
world of flowers.

TO JOHN FORSTER.

WITH SHAKESPERE'S WORKS.

I DO not know a man who better reads
Or weighs the great thoughts of the book I send,—
Better than he whom I have called my friend
For twenty years and upwards. He who feeds
Upon Shakesperian pastures never needs
The humbler food which springs from plains below:
Yet may he love the little flowers that blow,
And him excuse who for their beauty pleads.

Take then my Shakespere to some sylvan nook;
And pray thee, in the name of Days of old,
Good-will and friendship, never bought or sold,
Give me assurance thou wilt always look
With kindness still on Spirits of humbler mould;
Kept firm by resting on that wondrous book,
Wherein the Dream of Life is all unrolled.

EPISTLE

FROM AN OBSCURE PHILOSOPHER.

PRONE on my bed, I send these lines to thee,
Ó Hieros! Strange dreams of days gone by
Haunt 'round my brain: Delights, and Pains, and Scenes
Peopled with pleasant shapes (now lost!) like ghosts
Across some crystal mirror, come and go;
I helpless! These give leisure to my days,
And nights, (which are not all involved and dark);
And so I purpose to redeem my pledge,
And tell thee briefly, my poor history.

Friend,—for thou art my friend, altho' we two
Have trod our different roads, from life to death;
Thou thro' the holy pastures, where the sheep,
Guided by croziered shepherds, feed at ease,
And drink the heavenly waters, and sleep safe;
I through the tangled wastes and briery depths,
Struggling, heart-sore, have found my way by night!

Well,—Thou hast often called me, I confess,
And told me of thy pleasant paths on high,
Beckoning me upwards. I *would* go my way;
For I believed my road led upwards too,

And had its verdant nooks, and daisied spots
Pearling the meadows, somewhere, — afar off!
So I wore onwards. I was near the goal,
Felt the fresh air, and saw the sunny steeps,
When suddenly came — Death! Then, Hope being fled,
I sank and strove no more.

Yet have I had
Delight in labor, as thou hadst in ease.
'Twas pleasant to endure, and know that I
Must conquer in the end. 'Twas pleasant, too,
To free my thoughts from parsimonious tasks,
And bid them seek the liberal air, and fly
(The larks!) up to the sun. They brought me down
Wealth that you care not for, perhaps despise;
Siderean music from the Pleiades;
Vast truths which soaring Science never reached;
Dim intimations from majestic Souls
Who died long since, and fled, we know not where,
And messages from all the Orbs of Heaven.

Had I but studied all my father taught,
I should have mastered every science; plunged
Deep in geometry and numbers; piled
Million on million; bale on bale; until
My iron rooms and bags had burst with gold.
He had a lust for gold, such as we see
For travel, where men leave their friends and homes,
And seek for unknown seas and desert sands.

But from my mother's lessons roses sprang;
Poured out their fragrance: lilies opened wide
Their breasts all dropt with gold: the winds, unsought,
Gave out fine meanings in each murmuring sound;
And those star-eyes, that fill the face of Night,
Shed on me all their mystic influence.

Thus dowered, I left the world to dig for gold,
Waste its worn youth, and write, with wrinkled brow,
Its sordid history; whilst I, emerging
Into the unpeopled air, where freedom was,
From my pure height saw all that Nature hoards
In silence for her faithful worshippers.
And what I sought I sought with all my soul;
For to do less is to ensure a loss;
As he who lazily seeks by some rope's length,
The dizzy height, and half-way loses his hold,
Falls down destroyed, because his heart is weak.
I suffered? — I rejoiced! as few have done,
In all the great extremes of happiness;
Nay, all those notes and shades of difference
That lie between the two points of excess,
Have each an individual self distinct
Pregnant with pleasure. Do you think I stood
Half-struck to marble, by those faultless forms
Dug out of Roman earth, without a pang
Of wonderful delight? I entered, wrapt,
Into the circle of Art; beheld (dismayed
By power) each one of Titian's master-works;

And rare Giorgione's sunset pastoral scenes,
Gleaming with gold ; the peerless perfect grace
That streams suffused thro' heavenly Raffaelle's forms, —
Child, virgin, matron, man, all near divine,
Half-earth, half-heaven ; and last those massive shapes
Which sprang from Michael's brain, and took their stand
Predominant, triumphant through all time ;
Whereat still youthful painters gaze with pride,
To think that Art hath done so much for men.

Leaving awhile these rainbow-colored paths,
I wandered through the flowery vales of sound,
Where Mozart wove, by night, his musk-rose airs ;
And thro' harmonious turns and labyrinths,
Where Handel once (with Galatea) strayed,
And Purcell, when he linked his soul to song.
From every grace I caught new light, new strength :
From radiant Art I rose to Poesy,
Which spread its wings across the warring heavens,
When he who sang the strife was old and blind ;
With Poesy, who upheld the Florentine,
When on his downward path he moved amazed ;
And who — when Nature bared her breast, and fed
Her wondrous Avon child, and in his ear
Poured all her secrets — bore him upwards, till
He touched the eternal stars and seemed to die !

At last, to Nature's self I turned, and read
Infinite marvels in her daily page.

I and all things on whom sweet life descends
Had intercourse. The insect that doth hold
His court upon a leaf, and dying yields
His generations to the sheltering grass,
Was my companion. In those April days,
Ere the rose opens, and when meadows burn
With flowers all colored like the morning beams,
And every point, thro' winter months left bare,
Pours out its buds, I made me friends, and grew
Familiar with the worm, and with the bird
That breeds its young within the guardian thorn.
—I tell these things, that thou mayst know there live,
Beyond the pulpit's velvet, and beyond
Thy lordly abbey, filled with meats and wines,
Things that belong to God; who sends their hearts
Upwards in fine melodious gratitude,
Leaving sweet lessons for poor men like me,
And some that even *thou* might'st deign to teach.
Something thou know'st, past knowledge, past all forms,
Dwells in the living breast. For with the gift
Of life is given the priceless dream of love,
And gratitude which pays to God who gives
Thanks beyond prayer. We, poor petitioners,
Too often content to ask, forget to pay
The debt we owe for good. Pardon us, Thou!
Infinite, Grand, Supreme Intelligence!
Teach us the lessons man was born to learn;
Lead us to loftier thoughts, to sunnier creeds;
For in the misty years of happiness,

Our hearts exhale with tenderest thoughts, which soar
Like dew from off the ground, and hallow us.

In the low hedge, hard by the open wilds,
The linnet builds her home; and in the roofs
Of populous towns the poor house-sparrow breeds:
Far from each other born, yet both alike
Become, by gentle usage, friends to those
Who seek and give them food and cherish them.
See where, aloft, upon the towering pine,
Broods the sea-eagle, and from year to year
Comes back unto her home of sedge and reeds,
And branches, interlaced with artist skill;
And hunts the seas by night, defends her young,
And, in all perils and all needs of life,
Shows strength beyond the strength of peasant minds.
In watchfulness, fidelity (beyond
Bribe or alarm), the household dog stands firm
In danger, when the faithful servant flies.
Wonderful knowledge, never learned from books!
Wonderful knowledge, from which man may learn
That he transcends not yet the bird or brute
In all things, — goodness, wisdom, gratitude.
Divinest Instinct, like the sun in air,
Thou reign'st unknown! — Unknown? Yet, as we talk,
The indefatigable Future comes,
Minute by minute, years by countless years;
These as they come, these legions, range about
The silent form of the Eternal Past,
Each with its scroll, from which all men may read.

My soul was calm; proud, haply, as I marked
Some finer lines, and truths half-hid that 'scape
The idler on the greensward ; and when Time
Led me to grander truths, and I beheld
What seemed the confluence of the stars, take shapes,
Grow into worlds, saw world encircling world,
Borne through their orbits by diviner powers,
And laws, that far outrun the thoughts of men,
Leaving the ground, my thoughts advanced, and took
Their stations near the sky, where angels dwell:
Thence — from this azure summit, built of air,
Descended suddenly an airier shape,
Swift as a sunbeam, tinged by hues of love.
Eyes that outshone the stars, and seemed to pierce
Beyond the secrets of remotest Time,
Looked down upon me, — *me!* Their luminous depths, —
Their grand sweet Silence, that surpassed all sound,
Held me like iron. I looked up, and wept, —
Wept, till soft words, bubbling through roses, rose
From inner fountains where the Soul abides,
And showered celestial balm. She stood disclosed,
A perfect soul within a perfect form ;
Unparalleled, intelligent, divine.
Dreams of some inner Heaven then took my soul
Captive, and flushed the thrilling nerves with joy,
Commingling with my sleep and blessing it;
And, when she warmed with love, my eyes amazed
Met thrice the wonders I before had seen:
I drank in fragrance thousand times more sweet

Than ever lay upon the hyacinth's lip :
Music I heard, sphere-tuned, harmonious,
Ravishing earth and sky : Swarms of delight
Encompassed me, until my soul o'erwhelmed
Sank in the conflict ; and I then poured forth
My heart in numbers such as lovers use : —

O perfect Love, soft Joy, untinged with pain !
O Sky, kept cloudless by the sighs of Spring !
O Bird, that bear'st sweet sounds thro' sun and rain,
Give thy heart way, and sing !

Look down, dear Love, as Heaven looks down on earth !
Be near me, round me, like the enfolding air !
Impart some beauty from thy beauteous worth ;
Or be thyself less fair.

As the hart panteth for the water-brooks ;
As the dove mourneth in the lone pine-tree ;
So, left unsunned by thy care-charming looks,
I pant, I mourn for thee !

— She came unto my home ; and with her came
Infinite love ; content ; divine repose.
Life rose above its height ; and we beheld
Beauty in all things, everywhere delight !
The Sun that dwelt in our own hearts shed forth
Its beams upon the world, and brightened it ;
And from that brightness, as the ground takes back

The dews it gently lends, we gathered light
That led us thro' the dim sweet paths of life,
Until our hearts bloomed forth in happiness.
—A home we had, not distant, yet removed
Somewhat aside from the laborious town,
Where friends (a few) would come when Spring had
touched
The sward with daisies. In our garden rose
Imperial cedars, underneath whose shade
We shunned the summer heat, and heard content
The little brook which ran and talked below.
Here 'twas at eve, we lingered, and saw rise
Those golden-crownèd daughters of the Night,
Who, when the sun is slumbering, take their place
And watch the world till morn, with sleepless eyes.
Behind us, in the distance, hills aspired
To mountains, on whose brows the early snow
Came and dwelt long; too far for cold; so near
We counted all the purple streaks that hung
O'er every misty valley. Oh how bright,
How filled with joy was all we looked upon!
Why should it end? . . .
. . . It ended. I am here,
Stripped of my wealth; alone. I am not shut
Out from the world like one that has no place,
But wander uncompanioned on my way.
Smit by a terrible doom, I yet look back
On things that charmed me once; that soothe me now.
The Day has faded. Evening still remains,

Wherein some deeds of good may yet be done.
I am not what I was: — that cannot be.
I could have lived without so fair a thing
To breathe beside me. But *she came*, and brought
That air which now is life. Without that air
I cannot live! I am a denizen
And dweller on an orb unknown before;
But now my natural soil; my only earth.
Ah! whilst I stood and gazed, out of the grass,
Out of the very flowers the serpent rose,
And in his labyrinthine sinewy coil
Strangled my earthly bliss! ——
But I forget.
A cloud came o'er me: it has passed away.
There is a Morning somewhere. Somewhere still
The Sun ascends his pathway as of old,
And light, and warmth, and beauty breathe again.
There will I go, should pain once leave me free:
If not, and I must close my journey here,
Content at last I rest. No cruel creed
Has bade me fire the martyr's blazing pile:
I have not trampled on the poor; nor made
My friend a footstool for myself to rise:
No outrage of another's tender thoughts,
No bland deceit that leads weak souls astray,
Was mine. My hours passed onwards without harm.
A few have bent the knee and deemed me kind:
I followed but my nature; nothing more.
Perhaps 'twas this which forced my bosom heave

With gratitude to God for all he gave;
That thrust my hand out tow'rds my fellow men,
And proffer comfort.
                    What is done is done!
And what is left? The Past, — the grave wise Past!
Of that I write — these few last words — to thee.

LE SCÉLÉRAT.

STILL are you here, a poisonous life
Outbreathing?
Still are you bands of deadly strife
Enwreathing?

Your friends, are they now foes? grown old
And stronger?
Your gold, is that all spent? *Your* gold
No longer?

Your thoughts that were so low, so blanched
By care,
Are they now buoyant, rose-like, launched
In air?

No! On your shoulder still that freak
Of birth,
(The hump,) still reigns, and bids you seek
The earth.

No! You help none, please none; nor love,
Nor give:
How is it, O slave, you dare to move?
To live?

Vile Shame! usurping still in space
A part,
Which else might own some earthly grace;
—Depart!

Thou, who ne'er earn'dst beneath Heaven's dome
A friend,
Into the black abyss, thy home,
Descend!

THE VICTOR.

He is dead, — whom I trusted and loved
In my innocent youth;
Gave my heart to, — in times when I knew not
A lie from a truth.

I gave him my all; the things hid
In the cells of my heart;
My wealth: would you know what he did
For my good, on his part?

He robbed me — he might have had all:
He smote me, — in vain:
I arose from the shock of my fall,
From the depths of my pain;

And I cried — "You have wronged me: — My life,
Love, and friendship I gave.
When you trembled and shrieked in the strife,
I was near you, to save.

But you stole from my arms the one prize
(Of my soul) that I won;
You ravished the light from my eyes,
The warmth from my sun:

So I slew you. In open mid-day,
  We met on the shore,
Where we met when our spirits were gay,
  And all life was before.

I slew you — in open fair fight:
  I clove thro' the brain
That so long had bewildered my sight;
  That had stung me to pain.

I saw you, still firm in my wrath,
  Fall dead on the sand;
And the last bloody (white and red) froth
  Bubbled warm on my hand.

And now? do you sleep? Are you yet
  In the pangs of your guilt?
For me, I have found no regret
  For the blood I have spilt.

I enjoy, on the sands where we fought,
  The fresh songs of the sea;
And I laugh, that my heart feeleth nought
  Of poor pity for thee."

THE KING IS DEAD.

I.

Sound the great bell!
The King of all the land is cold and dead:
He whom ye knew so well —
Know he hath nought whereon to rest his head,
Now, but the barest stone,
Whereon he lies alone,
Far from all help; life, love, and friendship — fled!

II.

Sound the great bell!
He whom ye knew in all his radiant power,
The wonder and pageant of an hour,
Has bade the world farewell;
Let slip his sceptre, doffed his crimson state;
And they, who at his pleasure used to wait,
Carp at his deeds, and tell
The wrongs he did to all, — his queenly mate,
Friends, foes, to Truth, to rank, and every ghost of state.

III.

Some future day, not far,
They'll build a column on the mountain near;

And in some pander rhyme,
Shape out historian lies for after-time.
Meanwhile, enlightened by a steadfast star,
I will set down,
In words that may be read by rich and poor,
By all who did his iron rule endure,
The truth (for once) of one who wore a crown.

TO A MYTH.

JUDGE of words without a meaning;
Arbiter 'tween black and white;
Fusing all the shades of difference
Into day or into night.

Cunning, cheating, grim magician;
Plunderer both of age and youth;
Slave of forms and senseless customs;
Laugher at the light of truth.

Has my life, then, all been wasted,
Threading thy bewildering ways?
Have I lost the hopeful morning?
Spoiled the evening of my days?

Down, thou Shape of hair and ermine!
Quit thy high disgracèd place.
Down, and meet thy nobler brother,
Simple Justice, face to face.

See, with what a brightening aspect,
He divides the right from wrong;
Mark, how swift his sentence follows;
Mark, how all content the throng.

But *Thou* — swollen and paltry figure,
Blown with vanity, stuffed with straw,
Pander now, and now a Tyrant,
Dar'st thou call thyself — "The Law?"

Where is all the heaped confusion,
Whereat shrinking Truth repines?
Wordy nonsense? leagues of charges,
With their sixes turned to nines?

Where the ruinous, rascal pleadings,
Drenched with spite, and lies, and ire?
Twaddling trash, delays, devices?
— Quick, let's heap the funeral pyre!

Quick! Send here the fusty parchments,
Smeared and spoiled a million ways;
All the senseless, worthless rubbish:
Now then, — set them all ablaze!

VANITY FAIR.

WHO'LL sell me a drum or a trumpet?
Who'll buy? — here are colors, a pair:
Here's drink for all those who'll be soldiers,
(And a shilling) at Vanity Fair.

Here's a glass for an eye that don't need it;
A mask for a face that can stare;
And a place in a Railway Direction,
(And so much a-year, you may swear).

Here's a virgin, rich, frightful, and fifty;
Here's a lord, with his pockets all bare,
(A young giant,) — if only he's thrifty,
He's sure of a sale at the fair.

Will you sell me some health, you physician?
You, sir, with your head full of hair,
(Not your own) will you puzzle the plaintiff,
And set right my wrongs, at the fair?

Here's a place for Sir Jeremy's cousin;
He swore (as you know he can swear)
That my enemies bribed right and left, when
I came in a member for — where?

Here's my lady's own maid: — Is it ready,
The pension rewarding her care?
All secrets she knows, and is steady;
And is dumb — on a certain affair.

O father, why droopeth your daughter,
So young, yet so faded by care?
"She is come to be sold, my fine fellow,
Draw near! she's the prize of the fair."

And she, neither bashful nor forward,
With something of *ton* in her air?
O widow, unbosom your beauty;
I would tender soft words, did I dare;

But I dare not; — and so as the daylight
Is fading to eve, it is time
To cease, and be thinking of dinner,
And to change both our dress and the rhyme.

* * * * * * *

Come, good friends, take what's before you;
Meat and drink, and welcome warm:
Here's a health to them that bore you,
And a curse for him that means you harm.

Deeply dive into your pockets;
Count no silver, spare no gold;
Here is all the world of wonders,
Each thing to be bought and sold.

Friendship — who will bid for friendship ?
Honor — look, it may be bought:
Love — a rare and curious specimen,
Found where it was never sought.

But no need to show each article.
Here's a figure for your grounds!
Spirit show, if you've a particle:
Shall I say "a thousand pounds ?"

Look! She lives. Who bids? What beauty!
Mark the outline of her form!
Come, sirs, you have each a duty
Towards your country to perform.

Thank you, sir, — ten thousand — twenty —
Thirty — fifty — a hundred! There,
Gone! — Where shall the lot be sent t' you ?
'Tis the prize, sir, of the fair!

JACK TURPIN.

Jack Turpin, I have known you long:
My serving man were you of yore,
When I was young and you were strong:
But Age is knocking at your door,

And now your shanks are shrunk and thin;
And Time has forced your hands to shake;
(Or can 't be — beer relieved by gin,
Which for a cold you used to take?)

Once you were villein, I the knight:
I paid you with some pence or pounds;
You served me, fairly whilst in sight;
Not well when you were "out of bounds."

Dwarfed, doggèd, boastful, drunken, shrewd,
A mute by day, by night a sot,
How often would you come, imbrued
With drink, and do — you know not what.

You blacked my shoes, you brushed my coat,
When sober, duly every morn;
But oft I heard your quavering note;
And when I lashed you with my scorn,

You shrank, resented, blushed with ire,
Would mostly argue, always lied.
Such lies as gin and beer inspire
You uttered with a proper pride.

O bragging knave! Thou had'st a head
Was round, and like a cannon-ball,
And some limp hairs above it spread;
And eyes that pierced one like an awl;

So firm, so daring was your look,
So unabashed by all reproof;
I read you, as one reads a book,
For knowledge, and my own behoof.

The glittering cunning in those eyes,
The oily, thick, slow, struggling word,
The helpless smile, the frown so wise,
All these I daily saw and heard.

How the grand funeral filled your head;
How well you wove the weaver's knot;
What projects rose, and failed, and fled;
My work, meanwhile, being all forgot!

Yet, Jack! I would I saw you here:
I think that I should hire you still;
And you at night might have your beer,
And sometimes, even by day, your will.

For you were honest; dextrous too,
After a fashion; and I think
I might, in time, prevail on you
To — yes, perhaps — abstain from drink.

And then, I think some faults were mine;
That I in angry words was free,
Impatient, — loved my cup of wine,
Was idle, obstinate, — like thee.

So, let's cast up the long account,
And strike the balance. Does it lie
This way? or that? — Come, tell th' amount!
Alas! you know no more than I.

That double entry, strict and mean,
Jack Turpin, let him keep who can;
I cannot: nor have I ever seen
One fair account 'tween man and man.

OLD LOVE.

You left me: I left you: (trampled down).
Were we not wrenched, we two, apart,
When your father's rage and your mother's frown
Sent a sting and a spasm to either heart?

You married, to pamper a father's pride;
I sank to the furrow and ploughed the soil:
You were slandered and praised thro' the country wide;
I, quietly scorned, was forced to toil.

You floated, a cork on the topmost wave;
I fell, a stone on the rocks below:
You were driven about, too near your grave,
While I heard from my cavern the tempest blow.

But the tempest fell. It has left you—life:
It has freed you at last from a master stern.
No need to re-plunge in the stormy strife,
Or again the hard lesson of life to learn.

I am here who have loved you for twenty years.
You are poor: I am wealthy—in gold and land;
You have suffered your sorrow; I had my tears:
Peace cometh. I offer my horny hand,

My heart, and my fortune; all that's mine!
Life still has its evening;—but I have done:
If you love me, it is but to make a sign:
If not,—ah! you tremble, and—*you make none!*

No sign,—but a smile, like the spasm that ran
Thro' my bosom, now stingeth my heart with pain:
'Tis a pang!—but I rise up a wiser man,
And I turn to my brother, the plough, again.

A COMPLAINT.

The clouds are heavy: the night is flowing
Duskily over the Eastern sky;
Rains are falling; winds are moaning:
The river is echoing sigh for sigh.
Upon its banks is a maiden plaining;
A tale she telleth of grief and wrong;
And she utters, to lighten her sad love-burthen,
The words of a half-forgotten song.
"A false friend and a bitter foe
Is Love to all who love below:
Ah! what is the use of our summer dreaming,
If life must evermore end in woe?"

A single pause, and aside she turneth
And sendeth a thought to her father dead;
To her cottage home where her mother mourneth;
A thought to her childhood bright and fled.
Her voice it is sad and full of dread!
Hark!—it thrills over the darkening water,
Telling a tale of future slaughter,
Like the cry of the deer when the hound hath caught her.
"O Love! thou bitter foe
To all who too much love below:
Is death the end of our summer dreaming?
And life is it ever more filled with woe?"

A PETITION.

You who dwell in upper air,
Young and fair!
Here is one who loveth ; take her to your care.
Beauty and the light of honor
Wears she like a crown upon her,
Grace around her whitest neck is hung :
Music, sadder now than came
When seraphs touched her lips with flame,
Sigheth from her tongue ;
And her eyes that once were bright,
Dazzling on the aching sight,
Fading are, like summer evening fading into night.

Many love her, but her bosom
Warmeth unto one unknown ;
Knows he what a wondrous treasure
Back upon her heart is thrown ?
Or the pain beyond a measure
Borne for him alone ?
Bid him come, where'er he linger ;
Whisper in his charmèd ear,
What a sad sweet beauteous singer
Liveth, — dieth for him here.

You who dwell in upper air,
Fair and young, bright as fair,
Star-like, — lamp-like hung on high,
Angel stars that never die!
Disappearing, but returning,
In your constant season burning;
In the sightless ether hung,
Like to random jewels flung
On the forehead of the sky;
Look on her with all your brightness,
Bid her heart resume its lightness;
Tell her there are hopes above her,
Tell her of a world to love her,
Bind the sweet wreath Hope, that hath no thorn,
around her;
So may joys arise
And light her happy eyes,
Till Love hath kissed the bride, and orange blooms
have crowned her!

LIFE.

In our youth we learn; in our manhood act.
What more? Alas, what more
Is in all Life, Fiction, Fact,
Than to see and hear, toil and strive to soar,
    For evermore!
What doth Life contain? what doth bind us here,
    In its thorny round?
Is it Hope, — that fadeth? Is it wizard Fear
That enchains our spirits with its whispered sound?
    In what cavern drear
    Are Life's pleasures found,
    When — strewn like leaves around —
    Thousands pine and sigh
    For a home on high,
Some for gentle rest, beneath the daisied ground?

A WORD ON BEHALF OF WATER.

SENT TO MISS JULIA ——.

THE murmuring Water, — how it runs
Its seaward course, how pure and clear,
Past all the snows and all the suns
That lie within the Julian year.

Not dangerous, like the fiery wines;
Not turbid, like the drunken beer;
It lends its aid to all, and shines,
The glory of the Julian year.

Once, in my careless, thoughtless youth,
I sang of riotous vinous cheer;
But now I turn to simple Truth,
Taught — by two Julian stars — to steer.

By Julian stars I see the right,
By Julian stars I see the wrong,
And Julia, by her gentle might,
Now turns my humble prose — to song.

ON YORICK,

A LITTLE SPANIEL.

A LITTLE life has ended!
Our voices cease to call,
Our eyes to look for one who was
A favorite with us all.

We miss his eager movements,
His eyes of tender light:
There's something wanting to the Day,
And something to the Night.

Six years we loved and cherished him,
Six years he was our friend;
And we tried to make his little life
Run smoothly to the end.

A great and terrible Power
Came down and checked his breath:
It comes to Sages, Heroes, Kings,
And then we call it "DEATH."

It came without sound or warning.
A single, feeble cry
Told that the Shadow fell on him,
And time was come — to die!

For men unloved and meaner things
Let false vain boastings be;
This verse, my Yorick, shall remain
(An epitaph) for thee!

THE FISHER'S WIFE.

The clouds are heavy and dark,
The winds are abroad at sea,
And the thunder comes: — his minute-guns
Do they sound an alarm for me?

They say that the waves are still,
Are as calm as calm can be;
But I hear a shriek, as the waters break:
My God! does he die for me?

Oh, why did he leave us all,
And venture on such a sea!
It was still at home, but the boiling foam
Called out from afar, to me.

We have starved our whole life long:
Why not bear a little more?
'Twas better than send our one last friend
To die on the stormy shore.

If ever he come again,
Once safe from the murderous sea,
I will toil for aye, both night and day,
So he never need toil for me.

My bairns, they are clinging around:
They shout: Is it death they see?
What is it they mark in the coming dark?
I tremble — oh, Life! 'tis He.

SONG.

"Tell me what hath bound thee
To a life of pain:
Lovers all surround thee
With an amorous chain:
Why dost thou refuse? Why dost thou complain?

Knights and nobles sue thee
To become a bride;
Wealth and power woo thee
To their golden side:
Why dost thou refuse? from modesty? from pride?"

"I am seeking treasures
Such as angels gain, —
Pure untainted pleasures,
Thro' the world, in vain:
So I still refuse, — so I still complain."

SISTERS OF MUSIC.

"Who sings?" said the Spirit of Music,
And smiled on her peers:
"Sweet *Sorrow*, sing Thou!" Sorrow answered,
"I cannot — for tears."

"Bright *Hope*, give a tongue to the poems
I read in thine eyes."
Hope answered — "My thoughts are all clouded,
And lost in the skies."

"Then *Joy*, put thy mouth to the bugle!
A note for my sake."
Calm creature, she sleeps in the sunshine,
And will not awake.

But hush! a soft sound stealeth onwards,
Like the flight of a dove;
Ah, I find that the Song that is sweetest
Comes ever from *Love*.

THE SPOT OF GREEN.

When the winter bloweth loud,
And the earth is in a shroud,
Bitter rain and blinding snow
Dimming every dream below;
Cheerily! cheerily!
There is ever a spot of green,
Whence the Heavens may be seen.

When our purse is shrinking fast,
And our friend is lost (the last!),
And the world doth pour its pain
Sharper than the frozen rain;
Cheerily! cheerily!
There is still a spot of green,
Whence the Heavens may be seen.

Let us never greet despair,
While the little spot is there:
For Winter brighteneth into May,
And sullen Night to sunny Day;
So cheerily, cheerily!
Let us seek the spot of green,
Hopeful, patient, and serene,
Whence the Heavens may be seen.

PRISON POETRY.

Over the prison bars,
Over the walls so high,
Away unto the stars,
Flies the bird, Poesy!

No power can drown its notes;
No steel can clip its wings;
Beyond the mists it floats,
And soars, and sings;

Free, as the air is clear
From bar or bond or chain;
Its only prison here
In the Poet's brain!

AFTER DEATH.

Tread softly by this long, close-curtained room!
Within, reposing on her stateliest bed,
Lies one embowered in the velvet gloom;
A creature, — dead:
Lately how lovely, how beloved, how young!
Around her beauteous mouth, sweet eyes, and golden hair,

(Making the fair thrice fair,)
A poet's first and tenderest verse was flung.
Now she lies ghastly pale, stone-cold, quite hid
From balmy April and the fragrant air,
Upon the dark, green, silken coverlid;
Her limbs laid out to suit the coffin's shape;
Her palms upon her breast, —
At rest!

What cries escape, ——
What sounds come moaning from the chamber near?
Small voices as of children smite the ear
With pity; and grave notes of deeper grief;
And sobs, that bring relief
To hearts which else might break with too much woe, —
With thoughts of long ago,
Loss of all earthly joy, and sweet Love's overthrow!

POVERTY.

O Poverty! O Poverty!
Children all of Poverty!
Thou who tak'st thy humble stand
Trading in the public way!
Thou with needle in thy hand,
Toiling from the birth of morning
Till the death of day!

Thou who laborest in the harvest
For the wealthy farmer's gain !
Thou whose pen must run for ever,
(Ever in the merry vein,)
Thorough days and nights of pain !
Thou whom Hunger's talons clutch,
Or Palsy smiteth with her crutch !
Thou who seek'st the 'Spital's bed,
Stumbling o'er the quick and dead !
Beggar of the sightless eye,
Martyr of the wind and storm,
Brother of each passer-by,
Who doth bare his shrunken form
To the Winter's cruelty !
Thou, — whate'er thy shape or feature,
Or thy name unknown, or nature,
Natural child of Poverty !
Know — that there are they who give
Their pity to all things that live,
And suffer ; that in every heart
There is still a better part ;
That at last the winter yieldeth,
And the ice is conquered, — won
By the glory of the Sun ;
That the evil of the earth
Dieth in a nobler birth ;
That all sorrow and all pain
Are but travelling shadows vain,
Fading in the mists of Time,
Like the poet's passing rhyme !

THE ALL-SUFFICIENT.

You love the dark and I the fair.
You worship her, so dark and tall;
I love (how much I love) the small,
When all the shapely points are there,
Round and smooth, (kind Nature's care,)
And a walk that's like the waving air,
Or golden corn when winds are blowing,
And a voice like waters flowing;
An eye — what heed of blue or grey,
Or hazle, so all scorn 's away,
And there's just a touch 'tween sad and gay?
Let the mouth be — Oh, a mouth
Such as when a rose looks South,
Gathering silver drops that fall
From the clouds, that over all
Swim, as swans swim in a lake,
With a glory in their wake.

You love; I love; then, what heed? —
If we love, and love indeed,
Nothing else, friend, do we need.

EVENING SONG.

WHISPER low, whisper low!
Lovers now should come and go.
When the Evening star is nearest
Comes the kiss that's last and dearest:
Hush! The over-jealous moon
Will o'ertake us soon.

Whisper soft, whisper soft!
Like the air that stirs aloft.
Let thy murmuring softer be
Than the sighing of the tree.
Lovers now should come and go,
Gentlier than the water's flow.

Farewell! Farewell!
They who kiss must never tell.
In thine eyes I see a light
Breaks the darkness of the night:
Ah!— my lip is nearest thine;
Now is Life divine!

THE PAST.

MOURN for the Rose!
The Rose who left her vernal halls unblown;
And fronting all the winds with bosom bare,
Was overthrown!

Mourn for the Past!
The Past that was so pleasant once, so bright:
The Dawn, the Noon, before we felt the Eve
That brings the Night.

The temple falls,
And the bird buildeth in the ruined tower;
And we, who once were strong, are crumbling fast,
Power by Power!

No Life, no Love
Resumes its morning. What is past is past!
Ay even Time, if Hebrew songs be true,
Must die at last!

VAGUE WISHES.

I aspire!
Unto that which hath no shape;
Unto that which hath no sound;
High, — higher, — higher,
I ascend! I quit the ground,
The human earth where hearts abound;
Swifter than the Lightning's fire
I aspire!
Past the high clouds floating 'round,
Where the eagle is not found,
Past the million-starry choir
I aspire,
Unto some sublime Desire!

Wondrous Visions o'er me bend!
From the love of worth and beauty,
From the trust that marks a friend,
To the highest heights of Duty
I ascend!
Not for poor or selfish end,
Poet's crown, Pontiff's tiar,
I aspire!

Through the mist of foul opinions,
Flaming passions, sensual mire,
To the Mind's serene dominions
I aspire!

I aspire!
Dread or doubt shall never haunt
The music of my wingèd lyre;
Nothing shall my spirit daunt,
Not the strength, not the ire,
Not the diabolic vaunt
Of the Phantom vague and gaunt,
Who with eyes of fatal fire,
And his quiver of arrows dire,
Scares the world. Death, avaunt!
Know that even beyond the strife
Of Love and Hate, of Death and Life,
Higher ever, — ever higher,
I aspire!

LOVE FOR LOVE.

Not because of Beauty,
  Or thy golden dower,
Hast thou, sweet one, over me
  Such surpassing power.

Not thine eyes of April,
  Not thy rose-fed youth,
Not thy gentle ways and words
  Won my love and truth.

Not by all enchanted
  Do I bend the knee:
Sweet Heart, I love *thee* — because
  Thou so lovest *me*.

THE PHILOSOPHER'S SONG.

Tell me not that you forget
All our pleasant summer season,
When we had no dun or debt,
When we loved without a reason;
When the sky was sunny bright,
Music in the river flowing,
And the heart was ever light,
And the roses ever blowing.

Why should chance, or others' will,
Beggar-rags, or regal ermine,
Ever shape our good or ill,
Or our happy days determine?
We have hope within us, here,
Deep within the true heart's centre.
Why should envy, why should fear,
Why should poor ambition enter?

In his heart a man should reign,
King of all that stirs within it:
Idle pleasure, idler pain,
Should not have command a minute.
Drink, then, to the days of old;
Be it wine, or sober water:
Here's to thee, my friend of gold,
Thee, and—Ah! thy peerless daughter!

LOVE-BIRD.

WITHIN the chambers of her breast
Love lives and makes his downy nest,
Midst opening blooms and fragrant flowers,
And there he dreams away the hours: —
There let him rest!
Sometime hence, when the cuckoo sings,
I'll come by night and bind his wings,
Bind him, that he shall not roam
From his warm white virgin home.

Maiden of the summer season,
Angel of the rosy time,
Come! unless some graver reason
Bid thee scorn my rhyme;
Come, from thy serener height
On a golden crown descending, —
Come, ere Love hath taken flight!
And let thy stay be like the light,
When its glory hath no ending
In the Northern night!

HERMELIN.

Oh, Love is a sweet-winged thief,
Hermelin!
He stealeth the red from the rose's leaf,
My Hermelin.
He stealeth the light from the azure eye,
The heart from the bosom, and then we die,
Gentle, gentle Hermelin.

He seemed but a sweet-souled child,
Hermelin!
And we trusted his smile and his eyes so mild,
My Hermelin.
And we moulded his words to a daily song;
We trusted, — and ah, we have suffered wrong,
Gentle, gentle Hermelin!

So, bar out the sweet winged thief,
Hermelin!
Or your days will be dark and wild and brief,
My Hermelin:
And your spirit will fade, and your tender eye
Will vanish in tears, and — so you'll die,
Gentle, gentle Hermelin!

SONG.

Sick am I, sweet love, to-day;
Weary, wandering have I been,
Led astray by dreams and visions
Thro' the wild weird forest green.

Let thy white hand fall on me,
Gently, like the alighting dove,
Scarcely felt, yet bearing with it,
Oh! — a world of love!

Let thy smiles be mine, — and tears,
And kisses, crimsoning like the West,
When the sun and breezes tremble
In the rose's breast.

So shall I revive, — and sing,
As I sang when young and free,
All the tenderer notes dissolving
In a hymn to thee!

PAST AND PRESENT

HEARTS we had in our sunny youth,
Steps as light as the winds that flee ;
She was fair as the angel Truth ;
I — as fond as a boy could be.
Now,
Cloudy skies and the sullen showers
Have dimmed the pleasures that once were ours.

I had hope like a thought in June,
She had tears like an April rain ;
When she spoke, 'twas a song in tune,
When she sighed, 'twas a rose in pain.
Now,
Wintry winds and the stormy showers
Have scattered the sweets from songs and flowers :
Come, let us fly
To a distant sky,
And dwell where the summer may still be ours.

A COMMON CHARACTER.

I LOVE *him*, that man so true:
You love this, — our friend so pleasant,
With his cordons red and blue.
T'other? — 'Faith, he's but a peasant;

Yet I love him. In his eyes
Lying see I not, nor scorning,
But the lights within them rise,
Clear, and like an April morning:

Not too warm; nor yet too cold,
For, with but a little pressing,
He will show a heart of gold,
Past all Californian guessing.

Look! all virtues in him found,
Pierce the outer surface glowing,
Truth, Love, Courage, Knowledge sound,
And — a few errors, worth your knowing.

SONG FOR ALL SEASONS.

When March tempests smite the pine,
Straight I dream of thee and thine,
And Spring so soon to be:
When the sweet bee, hour by hour,
Rifles in the red-rose flower,
Still I sigh for thee:

For thy voice, methinks, is ringing
'Midst the little laborer's singing.
Busy Insect-Song,
Delving deep for honey treasure,
Making very toil a pleasure,
Runs its life along.

When the black wild Winter throws
His icy gauntlet down, and blows
His trumpet to the sea;
And the great Sea answers loud,
From his throne amid the cloud,
Still I think on thee.

In the departing Summer's night,
And when the swallow takes her flight
Over land and sea,

And in Autumn storms and thunders,
Thro' the rain-dark misty wonders,
I look out for thee.

To every sound my Spirit wakes,
From every hue a color takes,
That brings me back to thee :
Ah ! when wilt thou, so deep in debt,
Thy scorn, and power, and pride forget,
And think, for once, of me ?

A QUESTION ANSWERED.

"Why do you love?"
"You ask me why?
'Tis for a look, a smile, a sigh;
A little look that no one notes,
A little sigh that hither floats,
And alights upon a tender heart.
Never felt I pang or smart
From that soft melodious thrilling,
That so stealeth round and round
My bosom. Not a single sound,
Harsher than a wood-dove's billing,
Wakes me from the dreams that creep
Through all my golden sleep.
Half asleep, half awake,
In the slumberous joy I slake
Thirst for knowledge, thirst for power;
Yielding, like a bending flower,
To the influence of the hour.
—Wherefore ask me why I love?
There are reasons here,—above
All your mathematic reckoning,
Smiles and looks (I told you) beckoning
Me from every old annoy,
Into the summer land of joy.

I leave behind the storm, the strife;
I bear with me the sun of life:
Imagination's wealth is mine:
The human has become divine:
I bask upon a faery shore:
I love: I am happy. Well! — what more?"

FORSAKE ME NOT.

Forsake me not, forsake me not,
When I am dead!
Leave me not, tho' life be fled,
But tend me to the last:
And tell me when my love is shed,
And my morn is overcast,
Shall I be by all forgot,
Like a flower whose stem is broken?
Ah, watch beside me, gentle maid,
Let me not in earth be laid,
Till a token
Be enwreathed around me,
Binding me to those who stay
Still beneath the sunny day;
Like the love that bound me
To your heart, so long ago;
When the phantom, Death, did call,
Whispering from beneath his pall,
With a voice 'tween joy and woe,
Long ago! long ago!

FROM THE LAMP.

FEED me with the fragrant oil,
Lest I fade; lest I die!
In my brazen home I toil
From the dusk till morn is nigh,
Lighting thee upon thy way,
So thou mayst not stop or stray,
As thou travellest alone
Through the starry lands unknown,
Or in regions where the streams
Of Poesy refine the brain
With sweet thoughts nectarean.
Often do I bring thee Dreams,—
Fairy Fancies, that in bands
Hither glide from haunted lands,
Where in deepest forest shade,
Love is nearest Wisdom laid;
Dreams, that, at the midnight drear,
Thou mayst in the silence hear,—
Sounds of silver trumpets blown,
Or the Viol's richest tone,
Drawn to fine ecstatic length,
By a master-artist's strength.

As a grain, refreshed in need,
Riseth from the buried seed

Into sweet requiting flowers,
Pleasant in the sultry hours;
Feed me now, and in return
I will rise and I will burn,
And will bear thee pleasant light
Through the darkness of the night.

TO THE LAMP.

In my youth I fed thee
With a learnèd oil;
In my manhood bred thee
To a life of toil.

What has been thy glory,
Under star or sun?
Tell me all thy story;
All that thou hast won.

Nothing! — Thou didst slumber
Through the wastes of time,
Or but help to cumber
Leaves with idle rhyme.

All our poet-treasure,
Coin by coin, is strung.
Let us part: — The measure
Of the song is sung!

A FAREWELL TO VERSE.

Sweet Muse! my friend of many years, — Farewell!
Sweet Mistress, who did never do me wrong;
But still with me hast been content to dwell
Through summer days and winter evenings long;
Sweet Nurse, whose murmur soothed my soul, Farewell!
I part with thee at last, — and with thy song!

Never again, unless some Spirit of might,
That will not be denied, command my pen,
Never again shall I essay to write
What thou (I thought!) didst prompt: Never again
Lose me in dreams until the morning light,
Or soar with thee beyond the worlds of men.

Farewell! — The plumage drops from off my wing:
Life and its humbler tasks henceforth are mine!
The lark no longer down from Heaven doth bring
That music which, in youth, I deemed divine:
The winds are mute; the river dares not sing: —
Time lifts his hand, — and I obey the sign!

www.ingramcontent.com/pod-product-compliance
Lightning Source LLC
LaVergne TN
LVHW010130110826
845151LV00002B/321

* 9 7 8 1 4 2 5 5 3 9 6 9 6 *